Individuals with Disabilities Education Act

Handbook for Special Education Teachers and Parents

2004 Reauthorization

Second Edition

by
Ted H. Gordon, J.D.,M.B.A.

California Bar Association (Inactive Member)
Adjunct Professor (Emeritus), Golden Gate University, San Francisco

CreateSpace, Charleston, South Carolina
https://www.createspace.com/4406644

ISBN-13:   978-1492186922
ISBN-10:   1492186929

Printed in the United States

To Madison, a wonderful 5^1/$_2$ year-old bundle of joy and love.

Table of Contents

504 Plans and Law

Behavioral Intervention

FORWARD

(This is a letter I wrote to a student using the first edition of this book explaining why cases are so important in the learning process.)

February 2, 2011

Dear [Name Omitted]

Thank you for your kind words about the value of my law book, and especially for taking the initiative to write and ask about why the book includes case examples among its pages. It's a good question, and the cases are one of the aspects that distinguish my book from the competition.

It is difficult learning about a subject that is so circumscribed and bound together by state and federal laws from such an inanimate object as a book.

The value of the course you are taking is not what grade you get in the class, but how well you are able to apply the principles to your life five years after the class is over.

I (and all the law schools in America and England) have found that such knowledge of legal principles can only be acquired by actually seeing the law applied to actual cases. It makes you think, helps you comprehend how the abstract principles of law actually apply to a real world situation, and assists you in analyzing how the law might apply to a real problem.

I have a Masters of Business Administration, which degree I earned before going to law school. In undergraduate business, it was easy to memorize the 16 principles of good management, the 9 qualities of human resources, etc. However, for my first test in my first class in the M.B.A. program, the professor gave us an example of a case (a real problem faced by a real company) and asked us to how we would advise the president of that company to respond.

The test results were interesting. The students who broadly paraphrased the 16 principles of good management, etc. received a "F" grade, since the president wasn't looking for platitudes about general information, but instead, he was seeking specific information about what would actually help him solve his problem.

This approach made us students rummage through all the information we had learned in undergraduate management classes, decide what was relevant to this particular situation, and figure out how to apply that information to this specific situation. In other words, we could no longer regurgitate information we had memorized from pages in a book but had to apply that knowledge to a real situation.

Yes, the cases are much harder to read and analyze than the straight-forward text summarizing the law. Hopefully, reading the cases and the court's solution will help you, as a student, understand how the principles of law apply and will allow you to use the law to help make decisions about your particular situation should you face such in the future.

Finally, and perhaps most significantly, school districts respond less aggressively when confronted with a letter citing a case. They assume you engaged someone with legal knowledge to helped you write the correspondence.

Best wishes.
Ted Gordon

Part One
General Information

CHAPTER ONE

INTRODUCTION

This book provides a background for the special education teachers and for parents of children with special educational needs and the rights granted under the Individual with Disabilities Education Act ("IDEA"). Since special education students often benefit from section 504 plans and behavior modification plans, both of those topics are also discussed. For simplicity and readability, the term *parent* as used in this book includes parent, guardian, custodian and anyone else who has legal rights to make decisions about a child's education.

Goal of this Book

Special education law is a large, complex subject, and the purpose of this book is only to highlight certain areas of the law the author feels important in understanding the context in which the law operates. It lays a foundation for grasping the purpose of special education laws as well as a reference of where to search for greater detail.

The book was designed as a supplemental textbook for university graduate students in special education and for parents of students with special education needs. To broaden the scope of this book and include all the laws would defeat the purpose of this book. One of this book's strengths is its brevity.

The law controlling students with disabilities is broad and thorough, and special education teachers and a school must follow that law or face the risk of litigation. Additionally, parents of special education students not finding the schools providing what is required by statute may force the schools to offer such benefits to their child at the school's expense. Thus, both sides need to be aware that at times there are a built-in adversarial situation, limited school resources, and students who can "fall through the cracks." Advocacy is often the only remaining procedure for parents who have exhausted their other avenues, while the only protection schools have is knowing the law and what they can do to avoid putting themselves at risk.

Code Section Reference

Teachers and parents looking at the law, especially through the Internet where the full laws are listed by code section without an easy entry, will find research is a tedious process. For that reason, the first section of this book lists the code sections and subsections of IDEA as if it was an index. Terms are alphabetical and provide the code section, so the user will know exactly which section and subsection of the law to read. Finding the right code section is often one of the more difficult tasks facing a teacher or parent and the alphabetical listing can help.

Law Evolves by Court Cases

This book, as does any book on the law, has certain limitations. Law is a fast evolving subject, and each year thousands of court cases are decided. These cases interpret and define the law in various fact patterns. Some of those court cases are appealed and are published where they serve as *binding* precedent on lower courts in that jurisdiction and *persuasive* authority for courts in other states.

The most obvious question asked is why isn't every case decided relevant and binding. It must be officially published before a court case can be used by other courts. At the state level as a general statement, only decisions of the state's appellate courts are published. In the federal courts, just important opinions of the district court (the main trial court of the federal government) are published. Additionally, federal cases decided by the federal appellate courts are published.

However, when the cost of a jury trial and then an appeal often costs $100,000 to $250,000, it is easy to understand why such a small percent of the cases are ever appealed. In chapter nine's case, one knowledgeable source stated the school's attorneys' fee was one-quarter of a million dollars for the trial and appeal.

Cases not only help define the law but also aid in understanding how the legal principles apply. For example, the case cited by the author in chapter eight involves the case of parents forcing their school district to pay for their child to attend a private school and to cover the costs of transportation and meals. Similarly, the case in chapter nine involves a probationary teacher who was fired for advocating for her disabled students and won $1 million award from the school district.

Law Often Amended

Generally, the law of special education is governed and controlled by federal statutes, and that law can be amended at any time. The first edition of this book was written in December 2002, and revised and updated for a second edition in August 2013. However, the law is always changing, either through court cases, statutes, or regulations, so the reader must always expect the possibilities of newer law on the subject and research accordingly. Still, the core of the law generally remains the same.

A final Note and Disclaimer

The material in this booklet is for educational purposes only. It is not a treatise on the law nor is it intended to be relied upon in deciding the law. Additionally, an author's interpretation of the law is not only a matter of opinion (not fact).

The thousands of cases handed down each year can significantly change the import of the law from one year to the next. Although the law of one jurisdiction should be the same in any other jurisdiction, in actuality such is not always the case.

So while the federal statutes apply throughout the United States, court cases interpreting those statutes can vary. The fact presented of an individual case can greatly influence the manner in which the law is applied, and while the rule in any one situation may seem the same, the courts may find the variations in the facts warrant a different conclusion of law.

CHAPTER TWO

FOR FURTHER REFERENCE

(For IDEA)

To check for updates and amendments to the IDEA code, one of the many sources that can be used as of 2013 is *http://www.law. cornell.edu/uscode/text,* which gives you a current version of the law as of the date you conduct your research. IDEA is found in 20 USC §1400 et seq. (meaning §1400 and code sections following §1400).

In doing your research, it seems a bit awkward because code sections 1400 and following are actually located in Chapter 33. So, doing your website search, look for:

(1) Title 20 (Education), then

(2) Chapter 33 (Individuals with Disabilities Education Act). Now, select

(3) Subchapter I (General Provisions) and Subchapter II (Assistance For Education Of All Children With Disabilities). Finally, choose

(4) The individual code sections, themselves.

(For California)

California State Statutes And Implementing Regulations

The code sections in this book are to the federal Individuals With Disabilities Education Act (commonly referred to simply as "IDEA"). At the state level the Act is implemented through California's enactment of the IDEA (at Education Code §56000–56875) and of the regulations found in Title 5 of the California Code of Regulations (CCR §3000-3100 and CCR §4600-4671).

Internet Database Search

The California Department of Education maintains a database of the laws, regulations, and policy relating to special education. These laws can search by keyword or by code numbers. As of August 2013, the address of the website is ww.cde.ca.gov/re/lr/.

Downloadable List of State Laws

The California Department of Education, Special Education Division, has an extensive list of statutes on special education that can be searched and downloaded. As of August 2013, the address of the website is:
http://www.cde.ca.gov/sp/se/lr/

Telephone Support For Parents And Teachers

Parents, teachers and other relevant individuals are entitled to telephone support in finding technical assistance, resources, and rights about students with disabilities. As of August 2013, the California Department of Education phone number for the *Procedural Safeguards Referral Service* is (800) 926-0648.

PART II
IDEA CODE AND REGULATIONS

CHAPTER THREE

IDEA ALPHABETIZED INDEX

IDEA is not indexed in the statutes, so the index below is one written by the author. The hardest part of any research for the novice is ascertaining the applicable code section. For that reason, the author's index is quite lengthy and hopefully extremely helpful.

The index term is on the left and the code citation is on the right. The next few chapters contains the written code of IDEA; the code sections in this index refer to that code.

In referring the statute the code is found in volume 20 of the *United State Code*. Only the subsection of the code is listed below in the index. So if the index shows *§1415(b)(7)*, then the full citation of the correct code section would be cited as *20 USC §1415(b)(7)*.

<u>IDEA Code Section</u>

A

Adult rights, explain in
    IEP to 16 year old...................................... §144(d)(1)(A)(viii)
Attorney
    Notices given to attorney........................... §1415(b)(7)
    Right to attend IEP meeting .... §1415(b)(7)
Autism is a disability... §1401(3)(A)(i)

B

Blind child, IEP encouraged to use
    Braille materials .... §1414(d)(3)(B)(iii)

C

Child
    Age 3-5 program for................................ .. §1414(d)(2)(B)

D

E

F

G

H

I

L

M

N

O

CHAPTER FOUR

CODE FINDINGS AND PURPOSE FOR IDEA

Author's Note. The code sections below are taken verbatim from federal code. Some of the subsections have no text, which seems strange, but then, Congress, who passed and drafted the statute, sometimes seems bizarre in its drafting. The portions of the code section below is reproduced exactly as written. They are part of Title 20 *United States Code*, Section 1400.

INDIVIDUALS WITH DISABILITIES EDUCATION ACT
SECTION 1400

(c) **Findings [for IDEA]**. Congress finds the following:

(1) Disability is a natural part of the human experience and in no way diminishes the right of individuals to participate in or contribute to society. Improving educational results for children with disabilities is an essential element of our national policy of ensuring equality of opportunity, full participation, independent living, and economic self-sufficiency for individuals with disabilities.

(2) Before the date of enactment of the Education for All Handicapped Children Act of 1975 (Public Law 94–142), the educational needs of millions of children with disabilities were not being fully met because—

(A) the children did not receive appropriate educational services;

(B) the children were excluded entirely from the public school system and from being educated with their peers;

(C) undiagnosed disabilities prevented the children from having a successful educational experience; or

(D) a lack of adequate resources within the public school system forced families to find services outside the public school system.

(3) Since the enactment and implementation of the Education for All Handicapped Children Act of 1975, this chapter has been successful in ensuring children with disabilities and the families of such children access to a free appropriate public education and in improving educational results for children with disabilities.

(4) However, the implementation of this chapter has been impeded by low expectations, and an insufficient focus on applying replicable research on proven methods of teaching and learning for children with disabilities.

(5) Almost 30 years of research and experience has demonstrated that the education of children with disabilities can be made more effective by—

(A) having high expectations for such children and ensuring their access to the general education curriculum in the regular classroom, to the maximum extent possible, in order to—

(i) meet developmental goals and, to the maximum extent possible, the challenging expectations that have been established for all children; and

    (ii) be prepared to lead productive and indepen-
dent adult lives, to the maximum extent possible;

(B) strengthening the role and responsibility of parents
and ensuring that families of such children have
meaningful opportunities to participate in the education of their children at school and at home;

(C) coordinating this chapter with other local, educational service agency, State, and Federal school improvement efforts, including improvement efforts
under the Elementary and Secondary Education
Act of 1965 [20 U.S.C. 6301 et seq.], in order to
ensure that such children benefit from such efforts
and that special education can become a service for
such children rather than a place where such children are sent;

(D) providing appropriate special education and related services, and aids and supports in the regular
classroom, to such children, whenever appropriate;

(E) supporting high-quality, intensive preservice preparation and professional development for all personnel who work with children with disabilities in
order to ensure that such personnel have the skills
and knowledge necessary to improve the academic
achievement and functional performance of children with disabilities, including the use of scientifically based instructional practices, to the maximum
extent possible;

(F) providing incentives for whole-school approaches,
scientifically based early reading programs, positive
behavioral interventions and supports, and early in-
tervening services to reduce the need to label children as disabled in order to address the learning

and behavioral needs of such children;

(G) focusing resources on teaching and learning while reducing paperwork and requirements that do not assist in improving educational results; and

(H) supporting the development and use of technology, including assistive technology devices and assistive technology services, to maximize accessibility for children with disabilities.

(6) While States, local educational agencies, and educational service agencies are primarily responsible for providing an education for all children with disabilities, it is in the national interest that the Federal Government have a supporting role in assisting State and local efforts to educate children with disabilities in order to improve results for such children and to ensure equal protection of the law.

(7) A more equitable allocation of resources is essential for the Federal Government to meet its responsibility to provide an equal educational opportunity for all individuals.

(8) Parents and schools should be given expanded opportunities to resolve their disagreements in positive and constructive ways.

(9) Teachers, schools, local educational agencies, and States should be relieved of irrelevant and unnecessary paperwork burdens that do not lead to improved educational outcomes.

(10)

(A) The Federal Government must be responsive to the growing needs of an increasingly diverse society.

(B) America's ethnic profile is rapidly changing. In 2000, 1 of every 3 persons in the United States was a member of a minority group or was limited English proficient.

(C) Minority children comprise an increasing percentage of public school students.

(D) With such changing demographics, recruitment efforts for special education personnel should focus on increasing the participation of minorities in the teaching profession in order to provide appropriate role models with sufficient knowledge to address the special education needs of these students.

(11)

(A) The limited English proficient population is the fastest growing in our Nation, and the growth is occurring in many parts of our Nation.

(B) Studies have documented apparent discrepancies in the levels of referral and placement of limited English proficient children in special education.

(C) Such discrepancies pose a special challenge for special education in the referral of, assessment of, and provision of services for, our Nation's students from non-English language backgrounds.

(12)

(A) Greater efforts are needed to prevent the intensification of problems connected with mislabeling and high dropout rates among minority children with disabilities.

(B) More minority children continue to be served in special education than would be expected from the percentage of minority students in the general school population.

(C) African-American children are identified as having

intellectual disabilities and emotional disturbance at rates greater than their White counterparts.

(D) In the 1998–1999 school year, African-American children represented just 14.8 percent of the population aged 6 through 21, but comprised 20.2 percent of all children with disabilities.

(E) Studies have found that schools with predominately White students and teachers have placed disproportionately high numbers of their minority students into special education.

(13)

(A) As the number of minority students in special education increases, the number of minority teachers and related services personnel produced in colleges and universities continues to decrease.

(B) The opportunity for full participation by minority individuals, minority organizations, and Historically Black Colleges and Universities in awards for grants and contracts, boards of organizations receiving assistance under this chapter, peer review panels, and training of professionals in the area of special education is essential to obtain greater success in the education of minority children with disabilities.

(14) As the graduation rates for children with disabilities continue to climb, providing effective transition services to promote successful post-school employment or education is an important measure of accountability for children with disabilities.

(d) **Purposes.** The purposes of this chapter are—

(1)

(A) to ensure that all children with disabilities have

available to them a free appropriate public education that emphasizes special education and related services designed to meet their unique needs and prepare them for further education, employment, and independent living;

(B) to ensure that the rights of children with disabilities and parents of such children are protected; and

(C) to assist States, localities, educational service agencies, and Federal agencies to provide for the education of all children with disabilities;

(2) to assist States in the implementation of a statewide, comprehensive, coordinated, multidisciplinary, interagency system of early intervention services for infants and toddlers with disabilities and their families;

(3) to ensure that educators and parents have the necessary tools to improve educational results for children with disabilities by supporting system improvement activities; coordinated research and personnel preparation; coordinated technical assistance, dissemination, and support; and technology development and media services; and

(4) to assess, and ensure the effectiveness of, efforts to educate children with disabilities.

Chapter Five

Code of *Individual With Disabilities Education Act*

Author's Note. This chapter contains selected portions of statutes, and in most cases not the entire statute. The goal is to make this material easier to digest, and overly lengthy and infrequently used portions of the statutes only serve to compound the difficulty of leaning the highlights of the code. The statute is cited as Title 20 *United States Code, Section* 1400 et seq.

Section 20 *USC* 1414(d) governing IEPs is omitted from this chapter as it is covered in the next chapter of this book.

For ease of reading, no reference is made to indicate the sections of the codes that are omitted. As mentioned before, Congress sometimes pass laws that have just a paragraph heading and no text in their subsections, which are naturally reproduced accordingly here in this text.

20 *USC* § 1400 – Congressional Statements and Declarations

(a) **Short Title**. This chapter may be cited as the "Individuals with Disabilities Education Act."

20 USC § 1401 – Definitions

(3) **Child with a disability**

(A) **In general**. The term "child with a disability" means a child—

    (i)   with intellectual disabilities, hearing impairments (including deafness), speech or language impairments, visual impairments (including blindness), serious emotional disturbance (referred to in this chapter as "emotional disturbance"), orthopedic impairments, autism, traumatic brain injury, other health impairments, or specific learning disabilities; and

    (ii)   who, by reason thereof, needs special education and related services.

(B) **Child aged 3 through 9**. The term "child with a disability" for a child aged 3 through 9 (or any subset of that age range, including ages 3 through 5), may, at the discretion of the State and the local educational agency, include a child—

    (i)   experiencing developmental delays, as defined by the State and as measured by appropriate diagnostic instruments and procedures, in 1 or more of the following areas: physical development; cognitive development; communication development; social or emotional development; or adaptive development; and

    (ii)   who, by reason thereof, needs special education and related services.

(14) **Individualized education program; IEP**. The term "individualized education program" or "IEP" means a written statement for each child with a disability that is developed, reviewed, and revised in accordance with section 1414 (d) of this title.

(26) **Related services.**

(A) **In general.** The term "related services" means transportation, and such developmental, corrective, and other supportive services (including speech-language pathology and audiology services, interpreting services, psychological services, physical and occupational therapy, recreation, including therapeutic recreation, social work services, school nurse services designed to enable a child with a disability to receive a free appropriate public education as described in the individualized education program of the child, counseling services, including rehabilitation counseling, orientation and mobility services, and medical services, except that such medical services shall be for diagnostic and evaluation purposes only) as may be required to assist a child with a disability to benefit from special education, and includes the early identification and assessment of disabling conditions in children.

(B) **Exception**. The term does not include a medical device that is surgically implanted, or the replacement of such device.

(30) **Specific learning disability.**

(A) **In general**. The term "specific learning disability" means a disorder in one or more of the basic psychological processes involved in understanding or in using language, spoken or written, which disorder may manifest itself in the imperfect ability to listen, think, speak, read, write, spell, or do mathematical calculations.

(B) **Disorders included**. Such term includes such conditions as perceptual disabilities, brain injury, minimal brain dysfunction, dyslexia, and developmental aphasia.

(C) **Disorders not included**. Such term does not

include a learning problem that is primarily the result of visual, hearing, or motor disabilities, of intellectual disabilities, of emotional disturbance, or of environmental, cultural, or economic disadvantage.

20 USC § 1412(a) – Mainstreaming

(5) **Least restrictive environment.**

(A) **In general.** To the maximum extent appropriate, children with disabilities, including children in public or private institutions or other care facilities, are educated with children who are not disabled, and special classes, separate schooling, or other removal of children with disabilities from the regular educational environment occurs only when the nature or severity of the disability of a child is such that education in regular classes with the use of supplementary aids and services cannot be achieved satisfactorily.

(B) **Additional requirement.**

(i) **In general.** A State funding mechanism shall not result in placements that violate the requirements of subparagraph (A), and a State shall not use a funding mechanism by which the State distributes funds on the basis of the type of setting in which a child is served that will result in the failure to provide a child with a disability a free appropriate public education according to the unique needs of the child as described in the child's IEP.

(ii) **Assurance.** If the State does not have policies and procedures to ensure compliance with clause (i), the State shall provide the Secretary an assurance that the State will revise the funding mechanism as soon as feasible to ensure that such mechanism does not result in such placements.

20 USC § 1414 - Evaluations, eligibility determinations, individualized education programs, and educational placements

(a) **Evaluations, parental consent, and reevaluations**

   (1) **Initial evaluations**.

     (A) **In general**. A State educational agency, other State agency, or local educational agency shall conduct a full and individual initial evaluation in accordance with this paragraph and subsection (b), before the initial provision of special education and related services to a child with a disability under this subchapter.

     (B) **Request for initial evaluation**. Consistent with subparagraph (D), either a parent of a child, or a State educational agency, other State agency, or local educational agency may initiate a request for an initial evaluation to determine if the child is a child with a disability.

     (C) **Procedures**.

       (i) **In general**. Such initial evaluation shall consist of procedures—

         (I) to determine whether a child is a child with a disability (as defined in 1401 of this title) within 60 days of receiving parental consent for the evaluation, or, if the State establishes a timeframe within which the evaluation must be conducted, within such timeframe; and

(II)   to determine the educational needs of such child.

(ii)   **Exception**. The relevant timeframe in clause (i)(I) shall not apply to a local educational agency if—

(I)   a child enrolls in a school served by the local educational agency after the relevant timeframe in clause (i)(I) has begun and prior to a determination by the child's previous local educational agency as to whether the child is a child with a disability (as defined in section 1401 of this title), but only if the subsequent local educational agency is making sufficient progress to ensure a prompt completion of the evaluation, and the parent and subsequent local educational agency agree to a specific time when the evaluation will be completed; or

(II)   the parent of a child repeatedly fails or refuses to produce the child for the evaluation.

(D) **Parental consent**.

(i)   **In general**.

(I)   **Consent for initial evaluation**. The agency proposing to conduct an initial evaluation to determine if the child qualifies as a child with a disability as defined in section 1401 of this title shall obtain informed consent from the parent of such child before conducting the evaluation. Parental consent for evaluation shall not be construed as consent for placement for receipt of special education and related services.

(II) **Consent for services**. An agency that is responsible for making a free appropriate public education available to a child with a disability under this subchapter shall seek to obtain informed consent from the parent of such child before providing special education and related services to the child.

(ii) **Absence of consent**

(I) **For initial evaluation**. If the parent of such child does not provide consent for an initial evaluation under clause (i) (I), or the parent fails to respond to a request to provide the consent, the local educational agency may pursue the initial evaluation of the child by utilizing the procedures described in section 1415 of this title, except to the extent inconsistent with State law relating to such parental consent.

(II) **For services**. If the parent of such child refuses to consent to services under clause (i)(II), the local educational agency shall not provide special education and related services to the child by utilizing the procedures described in section 1415 of this title.

(III) **Effect on agency obligations**. If the parent of such child refuses to consent to the receipt of special education and related services, or the parent fails to respond to a request to provide such consent—

(aa)   the local educational agency shall not be considered to be in violation of the requirement to make available a free appropriate public education to the child for the failure to provide such child with the special education and related services for which the local educational agency requests such consent; and

(bb)   the local educational agency shall not be required to convene an IEP meeting or develop an IEP under this section for the child for the special education and related services for which the local educational agency requests such consent.

(iii) **Consent for wards of the State**

(I)   **In general**. If the child is a ward of the State and is not residing with the child's parent, the agency shall make reasonable efforts to obtain the informed consent from the parent (as defined in section 1401 of this title) of the child for an initial evaluation to determine whether the child is a child with a disability.

(II)   **Exception**. The agency shall not be required to obtain informed consent from the parent of a child for an initial evaluation to determine whether the child is a child with a disability if—

(aa)   despite reasonable efforts to do so, the agency cannot discover the whereabouts of the parent of the child;

(bb)   the rights of the parents of the child have been terminated in accordance with State law; or

(cc)   the rights of the parent to make educational decisions have been subrogated by a judge in accordance with State law and consent for an initial evaluation has been given by an individual appointed by the judge to represent the child.

(E) **Rule of construction**. The screening of a student by a teacher or specialist to determine appropriate instructional strategies for curriculum implementation shall not be considered to be an evaluation for eligibility for special education and related services.

(2) **Reevaluations**.

(A) **In general**. A local educational agency shall ensure that a reevaluation of each child with a disability is conducted in accordance with subsections (b) and (c)—

(i) if the local educational agency determines that the educational or related services needs, including improved academic achievement and functional performance, of the child warrant a reevaluation; or

(ii)   if the child's parents or teacher requests a re-evaluation.

(B)   **Limitation**. A reevaluation conducted under subparagraph (A) shall occur—

(i)   not more frequently than once a year, unless the parent and the local educational agency agree otherwise; and

(ii)   at least once every 3 years, unless the parent and the local educational agency agree that a reevaluation is unnecessary.

(b)   **Evaluation procedures**

(1)   **Notice**. The local educational agency shall provide notice to the parents of a child with a disability, in accordance with subsections (b)(3), (b)(4), and (c) of section 1415 of this title, that describes any evaluation procedures such agency proposes to conduct.

(2)   **Conduct of evaluation**. In conducting the evaluation, the local educational agency shall—

(A)   use a variety of assessment tools and strategies to gather relevant functional, developmental, and academic information, including information provided by the parent, that may assist in determining—

(i)   whether the child is a child with a disability; and

(ii)   the content of the child's individualized education program, including information related to enabling the child to be involved in and progress in the general education curriculum, or, for preschool children, to participate in appropriate activities;

(B) not use any single measure or assessment as the sole criterion for determining whether a child is a child with a disability or determining an appropriate educational program for the child; and

(C) use technically sound instruments that may assess the relative contribution of cognitive and behavioral factors, in addition to physical or developmental factors.

(3) **Additional requirements**. Each local educational agency shall ensure that—

(A) assessments and other evaluation materials used to assess a child under this section—

(i) are selected and administered so as not to be discriminatory on a racial or cultural basis;

(ii) are provided and administered in the language and form most likely to yield accurate information on what the child knows and can do academically, developmentally, and functionally, unless it is not feasible to so provide or administer;

(iii) are used for purposes for which the assessments or measures are valid and reliable;

(iv) are administered by trained and knowledgeable personnel; and

(v) are administered in accordance with any instructions provided by the producer of such assessments;

(B) the child is assessed in all areas of suspected disability;

(C) assessment tools and strategies that provide relevant information that directly assists persons in determining the educational needs of the child are provided; and

(D) assessments of children with disabilities who transfer from 1 school district to another school district in the same academic year are coordinated with such children's prior and subsequent schools, as necessary and as expeditiously as possible, to ensure prompt completion of full evaluations.

(4) **Determination of eligibility and educational need**. Upon completion of the administration of assessments and other evaluation measures—

(A) the determination of whether the child is a child with a disability as defined in section 1401 (3) of this title and the educational needs of the child shall be made by a team of qualified professionals and the parent of the child in accordance with paragraph (5); and

(B) a copy of the evaluation report and the documentation of determination of eligibility shall be given to the parent.

(5) **Special rule for eligibility determination**. In making a determination of eligibility under paragraph (4)(A), a child shall not be determined to be a child with a disability if the determinant factor for such determination is—

(A) lack of appropriate instruction in reading, including in the essential components of reading instruction (as defined in section 6368 (3) of this title);

(B) lack of instruction in math; or

(C) limited English proficiency.

(6) **Specific learning disabilities.**

(A) **In general**. Notwithstanding section 1406 (b) of this title, when determining whether a child has a specific learning disability as defined in section 1401 of this title, a local educational agency shall not be required to take into consideration whether a child has a severe discrepancy between achievement and intellectual ability in oral expression, listening comprehension, written expression, basic reading skill, reading comprehension, mathematical calculation, or mathematical reasoning.

(B) **Additional authority** In determining whether a child has a specific learning disability, a local educational agency may use a process that determines if the child responds to scientific, research-based intervention as a part of the evaluation procedures described in paragraphs (2) and (3).

(c) **Additional requirements for evaluation and reevaluations.**

(1) **Review of existing evaluation data**. As part of an initial evaluation (if appropriate) and as part of any reevaluation under this section, the IEP Team and other qualified professionals, as appropriate, shall—

(A) review existing evaluation data on the child, including—

(i) evaluations and information provided by the parents of the child;

(ii) current classroom-based, local, or State

assessments, and classroom based observations; and

(iii) observations by teachers and related services providers; and

(B) on the basis of that review, and input from the child's parents, identify what additional data, if any, are needed to determine—

    (i) whether the child is a child with a disability as defined in section 1401 (3) of this title, and the educational needs of the child, or, in case of a reevaluation of a child, whether the child continues to have such a disability and such educational needs;

    (ii) the present levels of academic achievement and related developmental needs of the child;

    (iii) whether the child needs special education and related services, or in the case of a reevaluation of a child, whether the child continues to need special education and related services; and

    (iv) whether any additions or modifications to the special education and related services are needed to enable the child to meet the measurable annual goals set out in the individualized education program of the child and to participate, as appropriate, in the general education curriculum.

(2) **Source of data**. The local educational agency shall administer such assessments and other evaluation measures as may be needed to produce the data identified by the IEP Team under paragraph (1)(B).

(3) **Parental consent**. Each local educational agency shall obtain informed parental consent, in accordance with subsection (a)(1)(D), prior to conducting any reevaluation of a child with a disability, except that such informed parental consent need not be obtained if the local educational agency can demonstrate that it had taken reasonable measures to obtain such consent and the child's parent has failed to respond.

(4) **Requirements if additional data are not needed**. If the IEP Team and other qualified professionals, as appropriate, determine that no additional data are needed to determine whether the child continues to be a child with a disability and to determine the child's educational needs, the local educational agency—

   (A) shall notify the child's parents of—

      (i) that determination and the reasons for the determination; and

      (ii) the right of such parents to request an assessment to determine whether the child continues to be a child with a disability and to determine the child's educational needs; and

   (B) shall not be required to conduct such an assessment unless requested to by the child's parents.

(5) **Evaluations before change in eligibility**.

   (A) **In general**. Except as provided in subparagraph (B), a local educational agency shall evaluate a child with a disability in accordance with this section before determining that the child is no longer a child with a disability.

   (B) **Exception**.

(i)   In general. The evaluation described in subparagraph (A) shall not be required before the termination of a child's eligibility under this subchapter due to graduation from secondary school with a regular diploma, or due to exceeding the age eligibility for a free appropriate public education under State law.

(ii)   **Summary of Performance**. For a child whose eligibility under this subchapter terminates under circumstances described in clause (i), a local educational agency shall provide the child with a summary of the child's academic achievement and functional performance, which shall include recommendations on how to assist the child in meeting the child's postsecondary goals.

(d) **Individualized education programs**. [Subsection (d), which related to IEPs, is covered in the next chapter of this book]

Chapter Six

Code Sections Specifically Governing IEPs

Author's Note. This chapter is one of the most important in the book and it should be memorized, or at the very least, thoroughly understood. The special education teacher must be familiar with all of the criteria and requirements of a good individualized education program ("IEP"). Conversely, as a parent of a student needing an IEP, you look for violations of the statute, and in part you read an IEP accordingly.

The statute is cited as Title 20 *United States Code, Section* 1414(d), (e), and (f) with the appropriate subsections added to the citation.

20 USC 1414(d) Individualized Education Programs

(d) **Individualized education programs**

  (1) **Definitions**. In this chapter:

   (A) **Individualized education program**.

     (i) **In general**. The term "individualized education program" or "IEP" means a written statement for each child with a disability that is developed, reviewed, and revised in accordance with this section and that includes—

(I)   a statement of the child's present levels of academic achievement and functional performance, including—

(aa)   how the child's disability affects the child's involvement and progress in the general education curriculum;

(bb)   for preschool children, as appropriate, how the disability affects the child's participation in appropriate activities; and

(cc)   for children with disabilities who take alternate assessments aligned to alternate achievement standards, a description of benchmarks or short-term objectives;

(II)   a statement of measurable annual goals, including academic and functional goals, designed to—

(aa)   meet the child's needs that result from the child's disability to enable the child to be involved in and make progress in the general education curriculum; and

(bb)   meet each of the child's other educational needs that result from the child's disability;

(III)   a description of how the child's progress toward meeting the annual goals described in subclause (II) will be measured and when periodic reports on the progress the child is making toward meeting the annual goals (such as through the use of quarterly or other periodic reports, concurrent with the issuance of report cards) will be provided;

(IV)   a statement of the special education and related services and supplementary aids and services, based on peer-reviewed research to the extent practicable, to be provided to the child, or on behalf of the child, and a statement of the program modifications or supports for school personnel that will be provided for the child—

    (aa)   to advance appropriately toward attaining the annual goals;

    (bb)   to be involved in and make progress in the general education curriculum in accordance with subclause (I) and to participate in extracurricular and other nonacademic activities; and

    (cc)   to be educated and participate with other children with disabilities and nondisabled children in the activities described in this subparagraph;

(V)   an explanation of the extent, if any, to which the child will not participate with nondisabled children in the regular class and in the activities described in subclause (IV)(cc);

(VI)

      (aa)   a statement of any individual appropriate accommodations that are necessary to measure the academic achievement and functional performance of the child on State and districtwide assessments consistent with section 1412 (a)(16)(A) of this title; and

      (bb)   if the IEP Team determines that the child shall take an alternate assessment on a particular State or districtwide assessment of student achievement, a statement of why—

      (AA)   the child cannot participate in the regular assessment; and

      (BB)   the particular alternate assessment selected is appropriate for the child;

(VII)   the projected date for the beginning of the services and modifications described in subclause (IV), and the anticipated frequency, location, and duration of those services and modifications; and

(VIII)   beginning not later than the first IEP to be in effect when the child is 16, and updated annually thereafter—

      (aa)   appropriate measurable postsecondary goals based upon age appropriate transition assessments related to training, education, employment, and, where appropriate, independent living skills;

(bb) the transition services (including courses of study) needed to assist the child in reaching those goals; and

(cc) beginning not later than 1 year before the child reaches the age of majority under State law, a statement that the child has been informed of the child's rights under this chapter, if any, that will transfer to the child on reaching the age of majority under section 1415 (m) of this title.

(ii) **Rule of construction**. Nothing in this section shall be construed to require—

(I) that additional information be included in a child's IEP beyond what is explicitly required in this section; and

(II) the IEP Team to include information under 1 component of a child's IEP that is already contained under another component of such IEP.

(B) **Individualized education program team**. The term "individualized education program team" or "IEP Team" means a group of individuals composed of—

(i) the parents of a child with a disability;

(ii) not less than 1 regular education teacher of

such child (if the child is, or may be, participating in the regular education environment);

(iii) not less than 1 special education teacher, or
where appropriate, not less than 1 special education provider of such child;

(iv) a representative of the local educational agency who—

(I)   is qualified to provide, or supervise the
provision of, specially designed instruction to meet the unique needs of children with disabilities;

(II)   is knowledgeable about the general education curriculum; and

(III)   is knowledgeable about the availability
of resources of the local educational
agency;

(v) an individual who can interpret the instructional implications of evaluation results, who
may be a member of the team described in
clauses (ii) through (vi);

(vi) at the discretion of the parent or the agency,
other individuals who have knowledge or special expertise regarding the child, including
related services personnel as appropriate; and

(vii) whenever appropriate, the child with a disability.

(C) **IEP Team attendance**.

(i)   **Attendance not necessary**. A member of
the IEP Team shall not be required to attend

an IEP meeting, in whole or in part, if the parent of a child with a disability and the local educational agency agree that the attendance of such member is not necessary because the member's area of the curriculum or related services is not being modified or discussed in the meeting.

(ii) **Excusable**. A member of the IEP Team may be excused from attending an IEP meeting, in whole or in part, when the meeting involves a modification to or discussion of the member's area of the curriculum or related services, if—

(I) the parent and the local educational agency consent to the excusal; and

(II) the member submits, in writing to the parent and the IEP Team, input into the development of the IEP prior to the meeting.

(iii) **Written agreement and consent required**. A parent's agreement under clause (i) and consent under clause (ii) shall be in writing.

(D) **IEP Team transition**. In the case of a child who was previously served under subchapter III, an invitation to the initial IEP meeting shall, at the request of the parent, be sent to the subchapter III service coordinator or other representatives of the subchapter III system to assist with the smooth transition of services.

(2) **Requirement that program be in effect.**

(A) **In general**. At the beginning of each school year, each local educational agency, State educational agency, or other State agency, as the case may be, shall have in effect, for each child with a disability in the agency's jurisdiction, an individualized education program, as defined in paragraph (1)(A).

(B) **Program for child aged 3 through 5**. In the case of a child with a disability aged 3 through 5 (or, at the discretion of the State educational agency, a 2-year-old child with a disability who will turn age 3 during the school year), the IEP Team shall consider the Individualized Family Service Plan that contains the material described in section 1436 of this title, and that is developed in accordance with this section, and the Individualized Family Service Plan may serve as the IEP of the child if using that plan as the IEP is—

   (i)   consistent with State policy; and

   (ii) agreed to by the agency and the child's parents.

(C) **Program for children who transfer school districts**.

   (i)   **In general**.

      (I)   **Transfer within the same State**. In the case of a child with a disability who transfers school districts within the same academic year, who enrolls in a new school, and who had an IEP that was in effect in the same State, the local educational agency shall provide such child with a free appropriate public education, including services comparable to those described in the previously held IEP, in consultation with the parents until such time as the local educational agency adopts the previously held IEP or develops, adopts, and implements a new IEP that is consistent with Federal and State law.

(II) **Transfer outside State**. In the case of a child with a disability who transfers school districts within the same academic year, who enrolls in a new school, and who had an IEP that was in effect in another State, the local educational agency shall provide such child with a free appropriate public education, including services comparable to those described in the previously held IEP, in consultation with the parents until such time as the local educational agency conducts an evaluation pursuant to subsection (a)(1), if determined to be necessary by such agency, and develops a new IEP, if appropriate, that is consistent with Federal and State law.

(ii) **Transmittal of records.** To facilitate the transition for a child described in clause (i)—

(I) the new school in which the child enrolls shall take reasonable steps to promptly obtain the child's records, including the IEP and supporting documents and any other records relating to the provision of special education or related services to the child, from the previous school in which the child was enrolled, pursuant to section 99.31(a)(2) of title 34, Code of Federal Regulations; and

(II) the previous school in which the child was enrolled shall take reasonable steps to promptly respond to such request from the new school.

(3) Development of IEP

(A) **In general**. In developing each child's IEP, the IEP Team, subject to subparagraph (C), shall consider—

(i) the strengths of the child;

(ii) the concerns of the parents for enhancing the education of their child;

(iii) the results of the initial evaluation or most recent evaluation of the child; and

(iv) the academic, developmental, and functional needs of the child.

(B) **Consideration of special factors**. The IEP Team shall—

(i) in the case of a child whose behavior impedes the child's learning or that of others, consider the use of positive behavioral interventions and supports, and other strategies, to address that behavior;

(ii) in the case of a child with limited English proficiency, consider the language needs of the child as such needs relate to the child's IEP;

(iii) in the case of a child who is blind or visually impaired, provide for instruction in Braille and the use of Braille unless the IEP Team determines, after an evaluation of the child's reading and writing skills, needs, and appropriate reading and writing media (including an evaluation of the child's future needs for instruction in Braille or the use of Braille), that instruction in Braille or the use of Braille is not appropriate for the child;

(iv) consider the communication needs of the child, and in the case of a child who is deaf or hard of hearing, consider the child's language and communication needs, opportunities for direct communications with peers and professional personnel in the child's language and communication mode, academic level, and full range of needs, including opportunities for direct instruction in the child's language and communication mode; and

(v) consider whether the child needs assistive technology devices and services.

(C) **Requirement with respect to regular education teacher.** A regular education teacher of the child, as a member of the IEP Team, shall, to the extent appropriate, participate in the development of the IEP of the child, including the determination of appropriate positive behavioral interventions and supports, and other strategies, and the determination of supplementary aids and services, program modifications, and support for school personnel consistent with paragraph (1)(A)(i)(IV).

(D) **Agreement**. In making changes to a child's IEP after the annual IEP meeting for a school year, the parent of a child with a disability and the local educational agency may agree not to convene an IEP meeting for the purposes of making such changes, and instead may develop a written document to amend or modify the child's current IEP.

(E) **Consolidation of IEP Team meetings**. To the

extent possible, the local educational agency shall encourage the consolidation of reevaluation meetings for the child and other IEP Team meetings for the child.

(F) **Amendments**. Changes to the IEP may be made either by the entire IEP Team or, as provided in subparagraph (D), by amending the IEP rather than by redrafting the entire IEP. Upon request, a parent shall be provided with a revised copy of the IEP with the amendments incorporated.

(4) Review and revision of IEP

(A) **In general**. The local educational agency shall ensure that, subject to subparagraph (B), the IEP Team—

(i) reviews the child's IEP periodically, but not less frequently than annually, to determine whether the annual goals for the child are being achieved; and

(ii) revises the IEP as appropriate to address—

(I) any lack of expected progress toward the annual goals and in the general education curriculum, where appropriate;

(II) the results of any reevaluation conducted under this section;

(III) information about the child provided to, or by, the parents, as described in subsection (c)(1)(B);

(IV) the child's anticipated needs; or

(V) other matters.

(B) **Requirement with respect to regular education teacher**. A regular education teacher of the child, as a member of the IEP Team, shall, consistent with paragraph (1)(C), participate in the review and revision of the IEP of the child.

(5) **Multi-year IEP demonstration.**

(A) **Pilot program**.

(i) **Purpose**. The purpose of this paragraph is to provide an opportunity for States to allow parents and local educational agencies the opportunity for long-term planning by offering the option of developing a comprehensive multi-year IEP, not to exceed 3 years, that is designed to coincide with the natural transition points for the child.

(ii) **Authorization**. In order to carry out the purpose of this paragraph, the Secretary is authorized to approve not more than 15 proposals from States to carry out the activity described in clause (i).

(iii) **Proposal.**

(I) **In general**. A State desiring to participate in the program under this paragraph shall submit a proposal to the Secretary at such time and in such manner as the Secretary may reasonably require.

(II) **Content**. The proposal shall include—

(aa) assurances that the development of a multi-year IEP under this paragraph is optional for parents;

(bb)   assurances that the parent is required to provide informed consent before a comprehensive multi-year IEP is developed;

(cc)   a list of required elements for each multi-year IEP, including—

    (AA)   measurable goals pursuant to paragraph (1)(A)(i)(II), coinciding with natural transition points for the child, that will enable the child to be involved in and make progress in the general education curriculum and that will meet the child's other needs that result from the child's disability; and

    (BB)   measurable annual goals for determining progress toward meeting the goals described in sub-item (AA); and

(dd)   a description of the process for the review and revision of each multi-year IEP, including—

    (AA)   a review by the IEP Team of the child's multi-year IEP at each of the child's natural transition points;

(BB) in years other than a child's natural transition points, an annual review of the child's IEP to determine the child's current levels of progress and whether the annual goals for the child are being achieved, and a requirement to amend the IEP, as appropriate, to enable the child to continue to meet the measurable goals set out in the IEP;

(CC) if the IEP Team determines on the basis of a review that the child is not making sufficient progress toward the goals described in the multi-year IEP, a requirement that the local educational agency shall ensure that the IEP Team carries out a more thorough review of the IEP in accordance with paragraph (4) within 30 calendar days; and

(DD) at the request of the parent, a requirement that the IEP Team shall conduct a review of the child's multi-year IEP rather than or subsequent to an annual review.

(B) **Report**. Beginning 2 years after December 3, 2004, the Secretary shall submit an annual report to the Committee on Education and the Workforce of the House of Representatives and the Committee on Health, Education, Labor, and Pensions of the Senate regarding the effectiveness of the program under this paragraph and any specific recommendations for broader implementation of such program, including—

   (i) reducing—

      (I) the paperwork burden on teachers, principals, administrators, and related service providers; and

      (II) noninstructional time spent by teachers in complying with this subchapter;

   (ii) enhancing longer-term educational planning;

   (iii) improving positive outcomes for children with disabilities;

   (iv) promoting collaboration between IEP Team members; and

   (v) ensuring satisfaction of family members.

(C) **Definition**. In this paragraph, the term "natural transition points" means those periods that are close in time to the transition of a child with a disability from preschool to elementary grades, from elementary grades to middle or junior high school grades, from middle or junior high school grades to secondary school grades, and from secondary school grades to post-secondary activities, but in no case a period longer than 3 years.

(6) **Failure to meet transition objectives.** If a participating agency, other than the local educational agency, fails to provide the transition services described in the IEP in accordance with paragraph (1)(A)(i)(VIII), the local educational agency shall reconvene the IEP Team to identify alternative strategies to meet the transition objectives for the child set out in the IEP.

(7) **Children with disabilities in adult prisons**.

(A) **In general.** The following requirements shall not apply to children with disabilities who are convicted as adults under State law and incarcerated in adult prisons:

(i) The requirements contained in section 1412 (a)(16) of this title and paragraph (1)(A)(i)(VI) (relating to participation of children with disabilities in general assessments).

(ii) The requirements of items (aa) and (bb) of paragraph (1)(A)(i)(VIII) (relating to transition planning and transition services), do not apply with respect to such children whose eligibility under this subchapter will end, because of such children's age, before such children will be released from prison.

(B) **Additional requirement.** If a child with a disability is convicted as an adult under State law and incarcerated in an adult prison, the child's IEP Team may modify the child's IEP or placement notwithstanding the requirements of sections [1] 1412(a)(5)(A) of this title and paragraph (1)(A) if the State has demonstrated a bona fide security or compelling penological interest that cannot otherwise be accommodated.

20 USC 1414 (F). ALTERNATIVE MEANS OF MEETING PARTICIPATION. When conducting **IEP** team [2] meetings and placement meetings pursuant to this section, section 1415 (e) of this title, and section 1415 (f)(1)(B) of this title, and carrying out administrative matters under section 1415 of this title (such as scheduling, exchange of witness lists, and status conferences), the parent of a child with a disability and a local educational agency may agree to use alternative means of meeting participation, such as video conferences and conference calls.

20 USC 1415 (B)(7). EDUCATIONAL PLACEMENTS. (A) Procedures that require either party, or the attorney representing a party, to provide due process complaint notice in accordance with subsection (c)(2) (which shall remain confidential).... (B) A requirement that a party may not have a due process hearing until the party, or the attorney representing the party, files a notice that meets the requirements of subparagraph (A)....

Appendix A to Part 300
Notice of Interpretation

to IDEA Act, Implementing Regulations
(2002 Version—Infrequently Updated)

For ease of reading there are no notations in the court decision to indicate material was omitted. Any additions by the author are enclosed in brackets. Headings are added by the author for convenience.

These questions and answers arose as an Appendix to the 1999 regulations issued by the Department of Education. It was based on the initial IDEA of 1997. For reasons unclear to the author, the appendix was not included with the 2006 regulations. Nevertheless, most of the questions and answers offer reliable guidance to issues involving IDEA. It is well worth reviewing even though the responses must be evaluated through comparison with the most current reauthorization of IDEA.

Interpretation of IEP and Other Selected Requirements under Part B of the Individuals with Disabilities Education Act (IDEA; Part B)

Authority: Part B of the Individuals with Disabilities Education Act (20 U.S.C. 1401, et seq.), unless otherwise noted.

Individualized Education Programs (IEPs) and Other Selected Implementation Issues

Introduction

The IEP requirements under Part B of the IDEA emphasize the importance of three core concepts: (1) the involvement and progress of each child with a disability in the general curriculum including addressing the unique needs that arise out of the child's disability; (2) the involvement of parents and students, together with regular and special education personnel, in making individual decisions to support each student's (child's) educational success, and (3) the preparation of students with disabilities for employment and other post-school activities.

The first three sections of this Appendix (I-III) provide guidance regarding the IEP requirements as they relate to the three core concepts described above. Section IV addresses other questions regarding the development and content of IEPs, including questions about the timelines and responsibility for developing and implementing IEPs, participation in IEP meetings, and IEP content. Section IV also addresses questions on other selected requirements under IDEA.

Involvement and Progress of Each Child With a Disability in the General Curriculum

In enacting the IDEA Amendments of 1997, the Congress found that research, demonstration, and practice over the past 20 years in special education and related disciplines have demonstrated that an effective educational system now and in the future must maintain high academic standards and clear performance goals for children with disabilities, consistent with the standards and expectations for all students in the educational system, and provide for appropriate and effective strategies and methods to ensure that students who are children with disabilities have maximum opportunities to achieve those standards and goals. [Section 651(a)(6)(A) of the Act.]

Accordingly, the evaluation and IEP provisions of Part B place great emphasis on the involvement and progress of children with disabilities in the general curriculum. (The term ``general curriculum,'' as used in these regulations, including this Appendix, refers to the curriculum that is used with nondisabled children.)

While the Act and regulations recognize that IEP teams must make individualized decisions about the special education and related services, and supplementary aids and services, provided to each child with a disability, they are driven by IDEA's strong preference that, to the maximum extent appropriate, children with disabilities be educated in regular classes with their nondisabled peers with appropriate supplementary aids and services.

In many cases, children with disabilities will need appropriate supports in order to successfully progress in the general curriculum, participate in State and district-wide assessment programs, achieve the measurable goals in their IEPs, and be educated together with their nondisabled peers. Accordingly, the Act requires the IEP team to determine, and the public agency to [FR Page 12471] provide, the accommodations, modifications, supports, and supplementary aids and services, needed by each child with a disability to successfully be involved in and progress in the general curriculum achieve the goals of the IEP, and successfully demonstrate his or her competencies in State and district-wide assessments.

1. Major IEP Requirements. What are the major Part B IEP requirements that govern the involvement and progress of children with disabilities in the general curriculum?

Present Levels of Educational Performance

Section 300.347(a)(1) requires that the IEP for each child with a disability include ``* * * a statement of the child's present levels of educational performance, including--(i) how the child's disability affects the child's involvement and progress in the general curriculum; or (ii) for preschool children, as appropriate, how the child's disability affects the child's participation in appropriate activities * * *'' (``Appropriate activities'' in this context refers to age-relevant developmental abilities or milestones that typically developing children of the same age would be performing or would have achieved.)

The IEP team's determination of how each child's disability affects the child's involvement and progress in the general curriculum is a primary consideration in the development of the child's IEP. In assessing children with disabilities, school districts may use a variety of assessment techniques to determine the extent to which these children can be involved and progress in the general curriculum, such as criterion-referenced tests, standard achievement tests, diagnostic tests, other tests, or any combination of the above.

The purpose of using these assessments is to determine the child's present levels of educational performance and areas of need arising from the child's disability so that approaches for ensuring the child's involvement and progress in the general curriculum and any needed adaptations or modifications to that curriculum can be identified.

Measurable Annual Goals, including Benchmarks or Short-term objectives

Measurable annual goals, including benchmarks or short-term objectives, are critical to the strategic planning process used to develop and implement the IEP for each child with a disability. Once the IEP team has developed measurable annual goals for a child, the team (1) can develop strategies that will be most effective in realizing those goals and (2) must develop either measurable, intermediate steps (short-term objectives) or major milestones (benchmarks) that will enable parents, students, and educators to monitor progress during the year, and, if appropriate, to revise the IEP consistent with the student's instructional needs.

The strong emphasis in Part B on linking the educational program of children with disabilities to the general curriculum is reflected in Sec. 300.347(a)(2), which requires that the IEP include: a statement of measurable annual goals, including benchmarks or short-term objectives, related to-- (i) meeting the child's needs that result from the child's disability to enable the child to be involved in and progress in the general curriculum; and (ii) meeting each of the child's other educational needs that result from the child's disability.

As noted above, each annual goal must include either short-term objectives or benchmarks. The purpose of both is to enable a child's teacher(s), parents, and others involved in developing and implementing the child's IEP, to gauge, at intermediate times during the year, how well the child is progressing toward achievement of the annual goal. IEP teams may continue to develop short-term instructional objectives, that generally break the skills described in the annual goal down into discrete components.

The revised statute and regulations also provide that, as an alternative, IEP teams may develop benchmarks, which can be thought of as describing the amount of progress the child is expected to make within specified segments of the year. Generally, benchmarks establish expected performance levels that allow for regular checks of progress that coincide with the reporting periods for informing parents of their child's progress toward achieving the annual goals. An IEP team may use either short term objectives or benchmarks or a combination of the two depending on the nature of the annual goals and the needs of the child.

Special Education and Related Services and Supplementary Aids and Services

The requirements regarding services provided to address a child's present levels of educational performance and to make progress toward the identified goals reinforce the emphasis on progress in the general curriculum, as well as maximizing the extent to which children with disabilities are educated with nondisabled children.

Section 300.347(a)(3) requires that the IEP include: a statement of the special education and related services and supplementary aids and services to be provided to the child, or on behalf of the child, and a statement of the program modifications or supports for school personnel that will be provided for the child-- (i) to advance appropriately toward attaining the annual goals; (ii) to be involved and progress in the general curriculum * * * and to participate in extracurricular and other nonacademic activities; and (iii) to be educated and participate with other children with disabilities and nondisabled children in [extracurricular and other nonacademic activities] * * * [Italics added.]

Extent to Which Child Will Participate With Nondisabled Children

Section 300.347(a)(4) requires that each child's IEP include ``An explanation of the extent, if any, to which the child will not participate with nondisabled children in the regular class and in [extracurricular and other nonacademic] activities * * *'' This is consistent with the least restrictive environment (LRE) provisions at Secs. 300.550-300.553, which include requirements that:

> (1) each child with a disability be educated with non-disabled children to the maximum extent appropriate (Sec. 300.550(b)(1));

> (2) each child with a disability be removed from the regular educational environment only when the nature or severity of the child's disability is such that education in regular classes with the use of supplementary aids and services cannot be achieved satisfactorily (Sec. 300.550(b)(1)); and

> (3) to the maximum extent appropriate to the child's needs, each child with a disability participates with nondisabled children in nonacademic and extracurricular services and activities (Sec. 300.553).

All services and educational placements under Part B must be individually determined in light of each child's unique abilities and needs, to reasonably promote the child's educational success. Placing children with disabilities in this manner should enable each disabled child to meet high expectations in the future.

Although Part B requires that a child with a disability not be removed from the regular educational environment if the child's education can be achieved satisfactorily in regular classes with the use of supplementary aids and services, Part B's LRE principle is intended to ensure that a child with a disability is served in a setting where the child can be educated successfully.

Even though IDEA does not mandate regular class placement for every disabled student, IDEA presumes that the first placement option considered for each disabled student by the student's placement team, which must include the parent, is the school the child would attend if not disabled, with appropriate supplementary aids and services to facilitate such placement.

Thus, before a disabled child can be placed outside of

the regular educational environment, the full range of supplementary aids and services that if provided would facilitate
the student's placement in the regular classroom setting must
be considered. Following that consideration, if a determination is made that particular disabled student cannot be educated satisfactorily in the regular educational environment,
even with the provision of appropriate supplementary aids
and services, that student then could be placed in a setting
other than the regular classroom. Later, if it becomes apparent that the child's IEP can be carried out in a less restrictive setting, with the provision of appropriate supplementary
aids and services, if needed, Part B would require that the
child's placement be changed from the more restrictive setting to a less restrictive setting.

In all cases, placement decisions must be individually
determined on the basis of each child's abilities and needs,
and not solely on factors such as category of disability, sig-
nificance of disability, availability of special education and
related services, configuration of the service delivery system,
availability of space, or administrative convenience. Rather,
each student's IEP forms the basis for the placement decision.

Further, a student need not fail in the regular classroom
before another placement can be considered. Conversely,
IDEA does not require that a student demonstrate achievement of a specific performance level as a prerequisite for
placement into a regular classroom. [FR Page 12472]

Participation in State or District-Wide Assessments of Student Achievement

Consistent with Sec. 300.138(a), which sets forth a presump-
tion that children with disabilities will be included in general State and district-wide assessment programs, and provided with appropriate accommodations if necessary, Sec.
300.347(a)(5) requires that the IEP for each student with a
disability include: ``(i) a statement of any individual modifications in the administration of State or district-wide assessments of student achievement that are needed in order for

the child to participate in the assessment; and (ii) if the IEP team determines that the child will not participate in a particular State or district-wide assessment of student achievement (or part of an assessment of student achievement), a statement of-- (A) Why that assessment is not appropriate for the child; and (B) How the child will be assessed."

Regular Education Teacher Participation in the Development, Review, and Revision of IEPs

Very often, regular education teachers play a central role in the education of children with disabilities (H. Rep. No. 105-95, p. 103 (1997); S. Rep. No. 105-17, p. 23 (1997)) and have important expertise regarding the general curriculum and the general education environment. Further, with the emphasis on involvement and progress in the general curriculum added by the IDEA Amendments of 1997, regular education teachers have an increasingly critical role (together with special education and related services personnel) in implementing the program of FAPE for most children with disabilities, as described in their IEPs.

Accordingly, the IDEA Amendments of 1997 added a requirement that each child's IEP team must include at least one regular education teacher of the child, if the child is, or may be, participating in the regular education environment (see Sec. 300.344(a)(2)). (See also Secs. 300.346(d) on the role of a regular education teacher in the development, review and revision of IEPs.)

2. Need To Address General Curriculum. Must a child's IEP address his or her involvement in the general curriculum, regardless of the nature and severity of the child's disability and the setting in which the child is educated?

Yes. The IEP for each child with a disability (including children who are educated in separate classrooms or schools) must address how the child will be involved and progress in the general curriculum. However, the Part B regulations recognize that some children have other educational needs resulting from their disability that also must be met, even though those needs are not directly linked to participation in the general curriculum.

Accordingly, Sec. 300.347(a)(1)(2) requires that each child's IEP include: A statement of measurable annual goals, including benchmarks or short-term objectives related to--(i) Meeting the child's needs that result from the child's disability to enable the child to be involved in and progress in the general curriculum; and (ii) meeting each of the child's other educational needs that result from the child's disability.

Thus, the IEP team for each child with a disability must make an individualized determination regarding (1) how the child will be involved and progress in the general curriculum and what needs that result from the child's disability must be met to facilitate that participation; (2) whether the child has any other educational needs resulting from his or her disability that also must be met; and (3) what special education and other services and supports must be described in the child's IEP to address both sets of needs (consistent with Sec. 300.347(a)).

For example, if the IEP team determines that in order for a child who is deaf to participate in the general curriculum he or she needs sign language and materials which reflect his or her language development, those needs (relating to the child's participation in the general curriculum) must be addressed in the child's IEP.

In addition, if the team determines that the child also needs to expand his or her vocabulary in sign language that service must also be addressed in the applicable components of the child's IEP. The IEP team may also wish to consider whether there is a need for members of the child's family to receive training in sign language in order for the child to receive FAPE.

3. Regular teacher Involvement. What must public agencies do to meet the requirements at Secs. 300.344(a)(2) and 300.346(d) regarding the participation of a ``regular education teacher'' in the development, review, and revision of IEPs, for children aged 3 through 5 who are receiving preschool special education services?

If a public agency provides ``regular education'' preschool services to non-disabled children, then the requirements of Secs. 300.344(a)(2) and 300.346(d) apply as they do in the case of older children with disabilities. If a public agency makes kindergarten available to nondisabled children, then a regular education kindergarten teacher could appropriately be the regular education teacher who would be a member of the IEP team, and, as appropriate, participate in IEP meetings, for a kindergarten-aged child who is, or may be, participating in the regular education environment.

If a public agency does not provide regular preschool education services to nondisabled children, the agency could designate an individual who, under State standards, is qualified to serve nondisabled children of the same age.

4. Areas Addressed In IEP. Must the measurable annual goals in a child's IEP address all areas of the general curriculum, or only those areas in which the child's involvement and progress are affected by the child's disability?

> Section 300.347(a)(2) requires that each child's IEP include ``A statement of measurable annual goals, including benchmarks or short- term objectives, related to--(i) meeting the child's needs that result from the child's disability to enable the child to be involved in and progress in the general curriculum * * *; and (ii) meeting each of the child's other educational needs that result from the child's disability. . . .''
>
> Thus, a public agency is not required to include in an IEP annual goals that relate to areas of the general curriculum in which the child's disability does not affect the child's ability to be involved in and progress in the general curriculum. If a child with a disability needs only modifications or accommodations in order to progress in an area of the general curriculum, the IEP does not need to include a goal for that area; however, the IEP would need to specify those modifications or accommodations. *[Author Gordon: Some modifications by newer laws.]*
>
> Public agencies often require all children, including chil-

dren with disabilities, to demonstrate mastery in a given area of the general curriculum before allowing them to progress to the next level or grade in that area. Thus, in order to ensure that each child with a disability can effectively demonstrate competencies in an applicable area of the general curriculum, it is important for the IEP team to consider the accommodations and modifications that the child needs to assist him or her in demonstrating progress in that area.

Involvement of Parents and Students

The Congressional Committee Reports on the IDEA Amendments of 1997 express the view that the Amendments provide an opportunity for strengthening the role of parents, and emphasize that one of the purposes of the Amendments is to expand opportunities for parents and key public agency staff (e.g., special education, related services, regular education, and early intervention service providers, and other personnel to work in new partnerships at both the State and local levels (H. Rep. 105-95, p. 82 (1997); S. Rep. No. 105-17, p. 4 and 5 (1997)). Accordingly, the IDEA Amendments of 1997 require that parents have an opportunity to participate in meetings with respect to the identification, evaluation, and educational placement of the child, and the provision of FAPE to the child. (Sec. 300.501(a)(2)).

Thus, parents must now be part of: (1) the group that determines what additional data are needed as part of an evaluation of their child (Sec. 300.533(a)(1)); (2) the team that determines their child's eligibility (Sec. 300.534(a)(1)); and (3) the group that makes decisions on the educational placement of their child (Sec. 300.501(c)).

In addition, the concerns of parents and the information that they provide regarding their children must be considered in developing and reviewing their children's IEPs (Secs. 300.343(c)(iii) and 300.346(a)(1)(i) and (b)); and the requirements for keeping parents informed about the educational progress of their children, particularly as it relates to their progress in the general curriculum, have been strengthened (Sec. 300.347(a)(7)). [*Author Gordon: The 2004 reauthorizations forced parents participation.*]

The IDEA Amendments of 1997 also contain provisions that greatly strengthen the involvement of students with disabilities in decisions regarding their own futures, to facilitate movement from school to post-school activities. For example, those amendments (1) retained, essentially verbatim, the ``transition services'' requirements from the IDEA Amendments of 1990 (which provide that a statement of needed transition services must be in the IEP of each student with a disability, beginning no later than age 16); and (2) significantly [FR Page 12473] expanded those provisions by adding a new annual requirement for the IEP to include ``transition planning'' activities for students beginning at age 14. (See section IV of this appendix for a description of the transition services requirements and definition.)

With respect to student involvement in decisions regarding transition services, Sec. 300.344(b) provides that (1) ``the public agency shall invite a student with a disability of any age to attend his or her IEP meeting if a purpose of the meeting will be the consideration of--(i) The student's transition services needs under Sec. 300.347(b) (1); or (ii) The needed transition services for the student under Sec. 300.347(b)(2); or (iii) Both;'' and (2) ``If the student does not attend the IEP meeting, the public agency shall take other steps to ensure that the student's preferences and interests are considered.'' (Sec. 300.344(b)(2)).

The IDEA Amendments of 1997 also give States the authority to elect to transfer the rights accorded to parents under Part B to each student with a disability upon reaching the age of majority under State law (if the student has not been determined incompetent under State law) (Sec. 300.517). (Part B requires that if the rights transfer to the student, the public agency must provide any notice required under Part B to both the student and the parents.)

If the State elects to provide for the transfer of rights from the parents to the student at the age of majority, the IEP must, beginning at least one year before a student reaches the age of majority under State law, include a statement that the student has been informed of any rights that will transfer to him or her upon reaching the age of majority. (Sec. 300.347(c)).

The IDEA Amendments of 1997 also permit, but do not require, States to establish a procedure for appointing the parent, or another appropriate individual if the parent is not available, to represent the educational interests of a student with a disability who has reached the age of majority under State law and has not been determined to be incompetent, but who is determined not to have the ability to provide informed consent with respect to his or her educational program.

5. Role Of parents In IEP. What is the role of the parents, including surrogate parents, in decisions regarding the educational program of their children?

> The parents of a child with a disability are expected to be equal participants along with school personnel, in developing, reviewing, and revising the IEP for their child. This is an active role in which the parents (1) provide critical information regarding the strengths of their child and express their concerns for enhancing the education of their child; (2) participate in discussions about the child's need for special education and related services and supplementary aids and services; and (3) join with the other participants in deciding how the child will be involved and progress in the general curriculum and participate in State and district-wide assessments, and what services the agency will provide to the child and in what setting.
>
> As previously noted in the introduction to section II of this Appendix, Part B specifically provides that parents of children with disabilities--

>> Have an opportunity to participate in meetings with respect to the identification, evaluation, and educational placement of their child, and the provision of FAPE to the child (including IEP meetings) (Secs. 300.501(b), 300.344(a)(1), and 300.517;

>> Be part of the groups that determine what additional data are needed as part of an evaluation of their child (Sec. 300.533(a)(1)), and determine their child's eligibility (Sec. 300.534(a)(1)) and educational placement (Sec. 300.501(c));

>> Have their concerns and the information that they provide regarding their child considered in develop-

ing and reviewing their child's IEPs (Secs. 300.343(c)
(iii) and 300.346(a)(1)(i) and (b)); and

Be regularly informed (by such means as periodic report cards), as specified in their child's IEP, at least as
often as parents are informed of their nondisabled
children's progress, of their child's progress toward
the annual goals in the IEP and the extent to which
that progress is sufficient to enable the child to achieve
the goals by the end of the year (Sec. 300.347(a)(7)).

A surrogate parent is a person appointed to represent the interests of a child with a disability in the educational decision-
making process when no parent (as defined at Sec. 300.20)
is known, the agency, after reasonable efforts, cannot locate
the child's parents, or the child is a ward of the State under
the laws of the State. A surrogate parent has all of the rights
and responsibilities of a parent under Part B (Sec. 300.515.)

6. Child Involvement In IEP. What are the Part B requirements regarding the participation of a student (child) with a disability in an IEP meeting?

If a purpose of an IEP meeting for a student with a disability
will be the consideration of the student's transition services
needs or needed transition services under Sec. 300.347(b)(1)
or (2), or both, the public agency must invite the student and,
as part of the notification to the parents of the IEP meeting,
inform the parents that the agency will invite the student to
the IEP meeting.

If the student does not attend, the public agency must
take other steps to ensure that the student's preferences and
interests are considered. (See Sec. 300.344(b)).

Section Sec. 300.517 permits, but does not require,
States to transfer procedural rights under Part B from the
parents to students with disabilities who reach the age of
majority under State law, if they have not been determined
to be incompetent under State law. If those rights are to be
transferred from the parents to the student, the public agen-

cy would be required to ensure that the student has the right to participate in IEP meetings set forth for parents in Sec. 300.345. However, at the discretion of the student or the public agency, the parents also could attend IEP meetings as ``* * * individuals who have knowledge or special expertise regarding the child * * *'' (see Sec. 300.344(a)(6)).

In other circumstances, a child with a disability may attend ``if appropriate.'' (Sec. 300.344(a)(7)). Generally, a child with a disability should attend the IEP meeting if the parent decides that it is appropriate for the child to do so. If possible, the agency and parents should discuss the appropriateness of the child's participation before a decision is made, in order to help the parents determine whether or not the child's attendance would be (1) helpful in developing the IEP or (2) directly beneficial to the child or both. The agency should inform the parents before each IEP meeting- -as part of notification under Sec. 300.345(a)(1)--that they may invite their child to participate.

7. Notification About IEP Attendees. Must the public agency inform the parents of who will be at the IEP meeting?

Yes. In notifying parents about the meeting, the agency ``must indicate the purpose, time, and location of the meeting, and who will be in attendance.'' (Sec. 300.345(b), italics added.) In addition, if a purpose of the IEP meeting will be the consideration of a student's transition services needs or needed transition services under Sec. 300.347(b)(1) or (2) or both, the notice must also inform the parents that the agency is inviting the student, and identify any other agency that will be invited to send a representative.

The public agency also must inform the parents of the right of the parents and the agency to invite other individuals who have knowledge or special expertise regarding the child, including related services personnel as appropriate to be members of the IEP team. (Sec. 300.345(b)(1)(ii).)

It also may be appropriate for the agency to ask the parents to inform the agency of any individuals the parents will be bringing to the meeting. Parents are encouraged to let the agency know whom they intend to bring. Such cooperation can facilitate arrangements for the meeting, and help ensure a productive, child-centered meeting.

8. Parents Get Copy IEP. Do parents have the right to a copy of their child's IEP?

Yes. Section 300.345(f) states that the public agency shall give the parent a copy of the IEP at no cost to the parent.

9. When Disagreement About IEP. What is a public agency's responsibility if it is not possible to reach consensus on what services should be included in a child's IEP?

The IEP meeting serves as a communication vehicle between parents and school personnel, and enables them, as equal participants, to make joint, informed decisions regarding the (1) child's needs and appropriate goals; (2) extent to which the child will be involved in the general curriculum and participate in the regular education environment and State and district-wide assessments; and (3) services needed to support that involvement and participation and to achieve agreed-upon goals.

Parents are considered equal partners with school personnel in making these decisions, and the IEP team must consider the parents' concerns and the information that they provide regarding their child in developing, reviewing, and revising IEPs (Secs. 300.343(c)(iii) and 300.346(a)(1) and (b)).

The IEP team should work toward consensus, but the public agency has ultimate responsibility to ensure that the IEP includes the services that the child needs in order to receive FAPE. It is not appropriate to make IEP decisions based upon a majority ``vote.'' If the team cannot reach consensus, the public agency must provide the parents [FR Page 12474] with prior written notice of the agency's proposals or refusals, or both, regarding the child's educational program, and the parents have the right to seek resolution of any disagreements by initiating an impartial due process hearing.

Every effort should be made to resolve differences between parents and school staff through voluntary mediation or some other informal step, without resort to a due process hearing. However, mediation or other informal procedures may not be used to deny or delay a parent's right to a due process hearing, or to deny any other rights afforded under Part B.

10. Notification To Parents Of Child's Progress.
Does Part B require that public agencies inform parents regarding the educational progress of their children with disabilities?

Yes. The Part B statute and regulations include a number of provisions to help ensure that parents are involved in decisions regarding, and are informed about, their child's educational progress, including the child's progress in the general curriculum.

First, the parents will be informed regarding their child's present levels of educational performance through the development of the IEP. Section 300.347(a)(1) requires that each IEP include: * * * A statement of the child's present levels of educational performance, including--(i) how the child's disability affects the child's involvement and progress in the general curriculum; or (ii) for preschool children, as appropriate, how the disability affects the child's participation in appropriate activities * * *

Further, Sec. 300.347(a)(7) sets forth new requirements for regularly informing parents about their child's educational progress, as regularly as parents of nondisabled children are informed of their child's progress. That section requires that the IEP include: A statement of--(i) How the child's progress toward the annual goals * * * will be measured; and (ii) how the child's parents will be regularly informed (by such means as periodic report cards), at least as often as parents are informed of their nondisabled children's progress, of--(A) their child's progress toward the annual goals; and (B) the extent to which that progress is sufficient to enable the child to achieve the goals by the end of the year.

One method that public agencies could use in meeting

this requirement would be to provide periodic report cards to the parents of students with disabilities that include both (1) the grading information provided for all children in the agency at the same intervals; and (2) the specific information required by Sec. 300.347(a)(7)(ii)(A) and (B).

Finally, the parents, as part of the IEP team, will participate at least once every 12 months in a review of their child's educational progress. Section 300.343(c) requires that a public agency initiate and conduct a meeting, at which the IEP team: * * * (1) Reviews the child's IEP periodically, but not less than annually to determine whether the annual goals for the child are being achieved; and (2) revises the IEP as appropriate to address--(i) any lack of expected progress toward the annual goals * * * and in the general curriculum, if appropriate; (ii) The results of any reevaluation * * *; (iii) Information about the child provided to, or by, the parents * * *; (iv) The child's anticipated needs; or (v) Other matters.

Preparing Students With Disabilities for Employment and Other Post-School Experiences

One of the primary purposes of the IDEA is to ``* * * ensure that all children with disabilities have available to them a free appropriate public education that emphasizes special education and related services designed to meet their unique needs and prepare them for employment and independent living * * *'' (Sec. 300.1(a)).

Section 701 of the Rehabilitation Act of 1973 describes the philosophy of independent living as including a philosophy of consumer control, peer support, self-help, self-determination, equal access, and individual and system advocacy, in order to maximize the leadership, empowerment, independence, and productivity of individuals with disabilities, and the integration and full inclusion of individuals with disabilities into the mainstream of American society. Because many students receiving services under IDEA will also receive services under the Rehabilitation Act, it is important, in planning for their future, to consider the impact of both statutes.

Similarly, one of the key purposes of the IDEA Amendments of 1997 was to ``promote improved educational results for children with disabilities through early intervention, preschool, and educational experiences that prepare them for later educational challenges and employment.'' (H. Rep. No. 105-95, p. 82 (1997); S. Rep. No. 105-17, p. 4 (1997)).

Thus, throughout their preschool, elementary, and secondary education, the IEPs for children with disabilities must, to the extent appropriate for each individual child, focus on providing instruction and experiences that enable the child to prepare himself or herself for later educational experiences and for post-school activities, including formal education, if appropriate, employment, and independent living. Many students with disabilities will obtain services through State vocational rehabilitation programs to ensure that their educational goals are effectively implemented in post- school activities. Services available through rehabilitation programs are consistent with the underlying purpose of IDEA.

Although preparation for adult life is a key component of FAPE throughout the educational experiences of students with disabilities, Part B sets forth specific requirements related to transition planning and transition services that must be implemented no later than ages 14 and 16, respectively, *[Author Gordon: 2004 reauthorization change to just age 16.]* and which require an intensified focus on that preparation as these students begin and prepare to complete their secondary education.

11. What must the IEP team do to meet the requirements that the IEP include ``a statement of * * * transition service needs'' beginning at age 14 (Sec. 300.347(b)(1)(i)),'' and a statement of needed transition services'' no later than age 16 (Sec. 300.347(b)(2)?

[Author Gordon: 2004 reauthorization changed age 14 to age 16, so read this question #11 accordingly.] Section 300.347(b)(1) requires that, beginning no later than age 14, each student's IEP include specific transition-related content, and, beginning no later than age 16, a statement of needed transition services:

> Beginning at age 14 and younger if appropriate, and updated annually, each student's IEP must include: ``* * * a statement of the transition service needs of the student under the applicable components of the student's IEP that focuses on the student's courses of study (such as participation in advanced-placement courses or a vocational education program)'' (Sec. 300.347(b)(1)(i)).

> Beginning at age 16 (or younger, if determined appropriate by the IEP team), each student's IEP must include: ``* * * a statement of needed transition services for the student, including, if appropriate, a statement of the interagency responsibilities or any needed linkages.'' (Sec. 300.347(b)(2)).

The Committee Reports on the IDEA Amendments of 1997 make clear that the requirement added to the statute in 1997 that beginning at age 14, and updated annually, the IEP include ``a statement of the transition service needs'' is ``* * * designed to augment, and not replace,'' the separate, preexisting requirement that the IEP include, ``* * * beginning at age 16 (or younger, if determined appropriate by the IEP team), a statement of needed transition services * * *'' (H. Rep. No. 105-95, p. 102 (1997); S. Rep. No. 105-17, p. 22 (1997)).

As clarified by the Reports, ``The purpose of [the requirement in Sec. 300.347(b)(1)(i)] is to focus attention on how the child's educational program can be planned to help the child make a successful transition to his or her goals for life after secondary school.'' (H. Rep. No. 105-95, pp. 101-102 (1997); S. Rep. No. 105-17, p. 22 (1997)).

The Reports further explain that ``[F]or example, for a child whose transition goal is a job, a transition service could be teaching the child how to get to the job site on public transportation.'' (H. Rep. No. 105-95, p. 102 (1997); S. Rep. No. 105-17, p. 22 (1997)).

Thus, beginning at age 14, the IEP team, in determining appropriate measurable annual goals (including benchmarks or short- term objectives) and services for a student, must determine what instruction and educational experiences will assist the student to prepare for transition from secondary education to post-secondary life.

The statement of transition service needs should relate directly to the student's goals beyond secondary education, and show how planned studies are linked to these goals. For example, a student interested in exploring a career in computer science may have a statement of transition services needs connected to technology course work, while another student's statement of transition services needs could describe why public bus transportation training is important for future independence in the community.

Although the focus of the transition planning process may shift as the student approaches graduation, the IEP team must discuss specific areas beginning at least at the age of 14 years and review these areas annually. As noted in the Committee Reports, a disproportionate number of students with disabilities drop out of school before they [FR Page 12475] complete their secondary education: ``Too many students with disabilities are failing courses and dropping out of school. Almost twice as many students with disabilities drop out as compared to students without disabilities.'' (H. Rep. No. 105-95, p. 85 (1997), S. Rep. No. 105-17, p. 5 (1997).)

To help reduce the number of students with disabilities that drop out, it is important that the IEP team work with each student with a disability and the student's family to select courses of study that will be meaningful to the student's future and motivate the student to complete his or her education.

This requirement is distinct from the requirement, at

Sec. 300.347(b)(2), that the IEP include: * * * beginning at age 16 (or younger, if determined appropriate by the IEP team), a statement of needed transition services for the child, including, if appropriate, a statement of the interagency responsibilities or any needed linkages.

The term ``transition services'' is defined at Sec. 300.29 to mean: * * * a coordinated set of activities for a student with a disability that--(1) Is designed within an outcome-oriented process, that promotes movement from school to post-school activities, including postsecondary education, vocational training, integrated employment (including supported employment), continuing and adult education, adult services, independent living, or community participation; (2) Is based on the individual student's needs, taking into account the student's preferences and interests; and (3) Includes--(i) Instruction; (ii) Related services; (iii) Community experiences; (iv) The development of employment and other post- school adult living objectives; and (v) If appropriate, acquisition of daily living skills and functional vocational evaluation.

Thus, while Sec. 300.347(b)(1) requires that the IEP team begin by age 14 to address the student's need for instruction that will assist the student to prepare for transition, the IEP must include by age 16 a statement of needed transition services under Sec. 300.347(b)(2) that includes a ``coordinated set of activities * * *, designed within an outcome-oriented process, that promotes movement from school to post-school activities * * *.'' (Sec. 300.29) Section 300.344(b)(3) further requires that, in implementing Sec. 300.347(b)(1), public agencies (in addition to required participants for all IEP meetings), must also invite a representative of any other agency that is likely to be responsible for providing or paying for transition services. Thus, Sec. 300.347(b)(2) requires a broader focus on coordination of services across, and linkages between, agencies beyond the SEA and LEA.

12. Must the IEP for each student with a disability, beginning no later than age 16, include all ``needed transition services,'' as identified by the IEP team

and consistent with the definition at Sec. 300.29, even if an agency other than the public agency will provide those services? What is the public agency's responsibility if another agency fails to provide agreed-upon transition services?

Section 300.347(b)(2) requires that the IEP for each child with a disability, beginning no later than age 16, or younger if determined appropriate by the IEP team, include all ``needed transition services,'' as identified by the IEP team and consistent with the definition at Sec. 300.29, regardless of whether the public agency or some other agency will provide those services. Section 300.347(b)(2) specifically requires that the statement of needed transition services include, ``* * * if appropriate, a statement of the interagency responsibilities or any needed linkages.''

Further, the IDEA Amendments of 1997 also permit an LEA to use up to five percent of the Part B funds it receives in any fiscal year in combination with other amounts, which must include amounts other than education funds, to develop and implement a coordinated services system. These funds may be used for activities such as: (1) linking IEPs under Part B and Individualized Family Service Plans (IFSPs) under Part C, with Individualized Service Plans developed under multiple Federal and State programs, such as Title I of the Rehabilitation Act; and (2) developing and implementing interagency financing strategies for the provision of services, including transition services under Part B.

The need to include, as part of a student's IEP, transition services to be provided by agencies other than the public agency is contemplated by Sec. 300.348(a), which specifies what the public agency must do if another agency participating in the development of the statement of needed transition services fails to provide a needed transition service that it had agreed to provide.

If an agreed-upon service by another agency is not provided, the public agency responsible for the student's education must implement alternative strategies to meet the student's needs. This requires that the public agency provide the services, or convene an IEP meeting as soon as possible to identify alternative strategies to meet the transition services objectives, and to revise the IEP accordingly.

Alternative strategies might include the identification of another funding source, referral to another agency, the public agency's identification of other district-wide or community resources that it can use to meet the student's identified needs appropriately, or a combination of these strategies. As emphasized by Sec. 300.348(b), however:

Nothing in [Part B] relieves any participating agency, including a State vocational rehabilitation agency, of the responsibility to provide or pay for any transition service that the agency would otherwise provide to students with disabilities who meet the eligibility criteria of that agency.

[Author Gordon: this last paragraph has been modified by the 2004 reauthorization.] However, the fact that an agency other than the public agency does not fulfill its responsibility does not relieve the public agency of its responsibility to ensure that FAPE is available to each student with a disability. (Section 300.142(b)(2) specifically requires that if an agency other than the LEA fails to provide or pay for a special education or related service (which could include a transition service), the LEA must, without delay, provide or pay for the service, and may then claim reimbursement from the agency that failed to provide or pay for the service.)

13. Under what circumstances must a public agency invite representatives from other agencies to an IEP meeting at which a child's need for transition services will be considered?

Section 300.344 requires that, ``In implementing the requirements of [Sec. 300.347(b)(1)(ii) requiring a statement of needed transition services], the public agency shall also invite a representative of any other agency that is likely to be responsible for providing or paying for transition services.''

To meet this requirement, the public agency must identify all agencies that are ``likely to be responsible for providing or paying for transition services'' for each student addressed by Sec. 300.347(b)(1), and must invite each of those agencies to the IEP meeting; and if an agency invited to send a representative to a meeting does not do so, the public agency must take other steps to obtain the participation of that agency in the planning of any transition services.

If, during the course of an IEP meeting, the team identifies additional agencies that are ``likely to be responsible for providing or paying for transition services'' for the student, the public agency must determine how it will meet the requirements of Sec. 300.344.

Other Questions Regarding the Development and Content of IEPs

14. For a child with a disability receiving special education for the first time, when must an IEP be developed--before or after the child begins to receive special education and related services?

Section 300.342(b)(1) requires that an IEP be ``in effect before special education and related services are provided to an eligible child * * *.''

The appropriate placement for a particular child with a disability cannot be determined until after decisions have been made about the child's needs and the services that the public agency will provide to meet those needs. These decisions must be made at the IEP meeting, and it would not be permissible first to place the child and then develop the IEP. Therefore, the IEP must be developed before placement. (Further, the child's placement must be based, among other factors, on the child's IEP.)

This requirement does not preclude temporarily placing an eligible child with a disability in a program as part of the evaluation process--before the IEP is finalized--to assist a public agency in determining the appropriate placement for the child. However, it is essential that the temporary placement not become the final placement before the IEP is finalized. In order to ensure that this does not happen, the State might consider requiring LEAs to take the following actions:

> a. Develop an interim IEP for the child that sets out the specific conditions and timelines for the trial placement. (See paragraph c, following.)

> b. Ensure that the parents agree to the interim placement before it is carried out, and that they are involved throughout the [FR Page 12476] process of developing, reviewing, and revising the child's IEP.

> c. Set a specific timeline (e.g., 30 days) for completing the evaluation, finalizing the IEP, and determining the appropriate placement for the child.

> d. Conduct an IEP meeting at the end of the trial period in order to finalize the child's IEP.

15. Who is responsible for ensuring the development of IEPs for children with disabilities served by a public agency other than an LEA?

The answer as to which public agency has direct responsibility for ensuring the development of IEPs for children with disabilities served by a public agency other than an LEA will vary from State to State, depending upon State law, policy, or practice.

The SEA *[State Educatinal Agency]* is ultimately responsible for ensuring that all Part B requirements, including the IEP requirements, are met for eligible children within the State, including those children served by a public agency other than an LEA.

Thus, the SEA must ensure that every eligible child with a disability in the State has FAPE available, regardless of which State or local agency is responsible for educating the child. (The only exception to this responsibility is that the SEA is not responsible for ensuring that FAPE is made available to children with disabilities who are convicted as adults under State law and incarcerated in adult prisons, if the State has assigned that responsibility to a public agency other than the SEA. (See Sec. 300.600(d)).

Although the SEA has flexibility in deciding the best means to meet this obligation (e.g., through interagency agreements), the SEA must ensure that no eligible child with a disability is denied FAPE due to jurisdictional disputes among agencies.

When an LEA is responsible for the education of a child with a disability, the LEA remains responsible for developing the child's IEP, regardless of the public or private school setting into which it places the child.

16. For a child placed out of State by an educational or non- educational State or local agency, is the placing or receiving State responsible for the child's IEP?

Regardless of the reason for the placement, the ``placing'' State is responsible for ensuring that the child's IEP is developed and that it is implemented. The determination of the specific agency in the placing State that is responsible for the child's IEP would be based on State law, policy, or practice. However, the SEA in the placing State is ultimately responsible for ensuring that the child has FAPE available.

17. If a disabled child has been receiving special education from one public agency and transfers to another public agency in the same State, must the new public agency develop an IEP before the child can be placed in a special education program?

If a child with a disability moves from one public agency to another in the same State, the State and its public agencies have an ongoing responsibility to ensure that FAPE is made available to that child. This means that if a child moves to another public agency the new agency is responsible for ensuring that the child has available special education and related services in conformity with an IEP.

The new public agency must ensure that the child has an IEP in effect before the agency can provide special education and related services. The new public agency may meet this responsibility by either adopting the IEP the former public agency developed for the child or by developing a new IEP for the child. (The new public agency is strongly encouraged to continue implementing the IEP developed by the former public agency, if appropriate, especially if the parents believe their child was progressing appropriately under that IEP.)

Before the child's IEP is finalized, the new public agency may provide interim services agreed to by both the parents and the new public agency. If the parents and the new public agency are unable to agree on an interim IEP and placement, the new public agency must implement the old IEP to the extent possible until a new IEP is developed and implemented.

In general, while the new public agency must conduct an IEP meeting, it would not be necessary if: (1) A copy of the child's current IEP is available; (2) the parents indicate that they are satisfied with the current IEP; and (3) the new public agency determines that the current IEP is appropriate and can be implemented as written.

If the child's current IEP is not available, or if either the new public agency or the parent believes that it is not appropriate, the new public agency must develop a new IEP through appropriate procedures within a short time after the child enrolls in the new public agency (normally, within one week). *[Author Gordon: Since 2004 it has been one month, and not one week.]*

18.   **What timelines apply to the development**

and implementation of an initial IEP for a child with a disability?

Section 300.343(b) requires each public agency to ensure that within a reasonable period of time following the agency's receipt of parent consent to an initial evaluation of a child, the child is evaluated and, if determined eligible, special education and related services are made available to the child in accordance with an IEP. The section further requires the agency to conduct a meeting to develop an IEP for the child within 30 days of determining that the child needs special education and related services.

Section 300.342(b)(2) provides that an IEP must be implemented as soon as possible following the meeting in which the IEP is developed.

19. Must a public agency hold separate meetings to determine a child's eligibility for special education and related services, develop the child's IEP, and determine the child's placement, or may the agency meet all of these requirements in a single meeting?

A public agency may, after a child is determined by ``a group of qualified professionals and the parent'' (see Sec. 300.534(a)(1)) to be a child with a disability, continue in the same meeting to develop an IEP for the child and then to determine the child's placement.

However, the public agency must ensure that it meets: (1) the requirements of Sec. 300.535 regarding eligibility decisions; (2) all of the Part B requirements regarding meetings to develop IEPs (including providing appropriate notification to the parents, consistent with the requirements of Secs. 300.345, 300.503, and 300.504, and ensuring that all the required team members participate in the development of the IEP, consistent with the requirements of Sec. 300.344;) and (3) ensuring that the placement is made by the required individuals, including the parent, as required by Secs. 300.552 and 300.501(c).

20. How frequently must a public agency conduct meetings to review, and, if appropriate, revise the IEP for each child with a disability?

A public agency must initiate and conduct meetings periodically, but at least once every twelve months, to review each child's IEP, in order to determine whether the annual goals for the child are being achieved, and to revise the IEP, as appropriate, to address: (a) Any lack of expected progress toward the annual goals and in the general curriculum, if appropriate; (b) the results of any reevaluation; (c) information about the child provided to, or by, the parents; (d) the child's anticipated needs; or (e) other matters (Sec. 300.343(c)).

A public agency also must ensure that an IEP is in effect for each child at the beginning of each school year (Sec. 300.342(a)). It may conduct IEP meetings at any time during the year.

However, if the agency conducts the IEP meeting prior to the beginning of the next school year, it must ensure that the IEP contains the necessary special education and related services and supplementary aids and services to ensure that the student's IEP can be appropriately implemented during the next school year. Otherwise, it would be necessary for the public agency to conduct another IEP meeting.

Although the public agency is responsible for determining when it is necessary to conduct an IEP meeting, the parents of a child with a disability have the right to request an IEP meeting at any time. For example, if the parents believe that the child is not progressing satisfactorily or that there is a problem with the child's current IEP, it would be appropriate for the parents to request an IEP meeting.

If a child's teacher feels that the child's IEP or placement is not appropriate for the child, the teacher should follow agency procedures with respect to: (1) calling or meeting with the parents or (2) requesting the agency to hold another IEP meeting to review the child's IEP.

The legislative history of Public Law 94-142 makes it clear that there should be as many meetings a year as any one child may need (121 Cong. Rec. S20428-29 (Nov. 19, 1975) (remarks of Senator Stafford)). Public agencies should grant any reasonable parent request for an IEP meeting. For example, if the parents question the adequacy of services that are provided while their child is suspended for short periods of time, it would be appropriate to convene an IEP meeting.

In general, if either a parent or a public agency believes that a required component of the student's IEP should be changed, the public agency must conduct an IEP meeting if it believes that a change in the IEP may be necessary to ensure the provision of FAPE.

If a parent requests an IEP meeting because the parent believes that a change is needed [FR Page 12477] in the provision of FAPE to the child or the educational placement of the child, and the agency refuses to convene an IEP meeting to determine whether such a change is needed, the agency must provide written notice to the parents of the refusal, including an explanation of why the agency has determined that conducting the meeting is not necessary to ensure the provision of FAPE to the student.

Under Sec. 300.507(a), the parents or agency may initiate a due process hearing at any time regarding any proposal or refusal regarding the identification, evaluation, or educational placement of the child, or the provision of FAPE to the child, and the public agency must inform parents about the availability of mediation.

21. May IEP meetings be audio- or video-tape-recorded?

Part B does not address the use of audio or video recording devices at IEP meetings, and no other Federal statute either authorizes or prohibits the recording of an IEP meeting by either a parent or a school official. Therefore, an SEA or public agency has the option to require, prohibit, limit, or otherwise regulate the use of recording devices at IEP meetings.

If a public agency has a policy that prohibits or limits the use of recording devices at IEP meetings, that policy must provide for exceptions if they are necessary to ensure that the parent understands the IEP or the IEP process or to implement other parental rights guaranteed under Part B. An SEA or school district that adopts a rule regulating the tape recording of IEP meetings also should ensure that it is uniformly applied.

Any recording of an IEP meeting that is maintained by the public agency is an ``education record,'' within the meaning of the Family Educational Rights and Privacy Act (``FERPA''; 20 U.S.C. 1232g), and would, therefore, be subject to the confidentiality requirements of the regulations under both FERPA (34 CFR part 99) and part B (Secs. 300.560-300.575).

Parents wishing to use audio or video recording devices at IEP meetings should consult State or local policies for further guidance.

22. Who can serve as the representative of the public agency at an IEP meeting?

The IEP team must include a representative of the public agency who: (a) is qualified to provide, or supervise the provision of, specially designed instruction to meet the unique needs of children with disabilities; (b) is knowledgeable about the general curriculum; and (c) is knowledgeable about the availability of resources of the public agency (Sec. 300.344(a) (4)).

Each public agency may determine which specific staff member will serve as the agency representative in a particular IEP meeting, so long as the individual meets these requirements. It is important, however, that the agency representative have the authority to commit agency resources and be able to ensure that whatever services are set out in the IEP will actually be provided.

A public agency may designate another public agency member of the IEP team to also serve as the agency representative, so long as that individual meets the requirements of Sec. 300.344(a)(4).

23. For a child with a disability being considered for initial provision of special education and related services, which teacher or teachers should attend the IEP meeting?

A child's IEP team must include at least one of the child's regular education teachers (if the child is, or may be participating in the regular education environment) and at least one of the child's special education teachers, or, if appropriate, at least one of the child's special education providers (Sec. 300.344(a)(2) and (3)).

Each IEP must include a statement of the present levels of educational performance, including a statement of how the child's disability affects the child's involvement and progress in the general curriculum (Sec. 300.347(a)(1)). At least one regular education teacher is a required member of the IEP team of a child who is, or may be, participating in the regular educational environment, regardless of the extent of that participation.

The requirements of Sec. 300.344(a)(3) can be met by either: (1) a special education teacher of the child; or (2) another special education provider of the child, such as a speech pathologist, physical or occupational therapist, etc., if the related service consists of specially designed instruction and is considered special education under applicable State standards.

Sometimes more than one meeting is necessary in order to finalize a child's IEP. In this process, if the special education teacher or special education provider who will be working with the child is identified, it would be useful to have that teacher or provider participate in the meeting with the parents and other members of the IEP team in finalizing the IEP. If this is not possible, the public agency must ensure that the teacher or provider has access to the child's IEP as soon as possible after it is finalized and before beginning to work with the child.

Further, (consistent with Sec. 300.342(b)), the public agency must ensure that each regular education teacher, special education teacher, related services provider and other service provider of an eligible child under this part (1) has access to the child's IEP, and (2) is informed of his or her specific responsibilities related to implementing the IEP, and of the specific accommodations, modifications, and supports that must be provided to the child in accordance with the IEP. This requirement is crucial to ensuring that each child receives FAPE in accordance with his or her IEP, and that the IEP is appropriately and effectively implemented.

24. What is the role of a regular education teacher in the development, review and revision of the IEP for a child who is, or may be, participating in the regular education environment?

As required by Sec. 300.344(a)(2), the IEP team for a child with a disability must include at least one regular education teacher of the child if the child is, or may be, participating in the regular education environment.

Section 300.346(d) further specifies that the regular education teacher of a child with a disability, as a member of the IEP team, must, to the extent appropriate, participate in the development, review, and revision of the child's IEP, including assisting in--(1) the determination of appropriate positive behavioral interventions and strategies for the child; and (2) the determination of supplementary aids and services, program modifications, and supports for school personnel that will be provided for the child, consistent with 300.347(a)(3) (Sec. 300.344(d)).

Thus, while a regular education teacher must be a member of the IEP team if the child is, or may be, participating in the regular education environment, the teacher need not (depending upon the child's needs and the purpose of the specific IEP team meeting) be required to participate in all decisions made as part of the meeting or to be present throughout the entire meeting or attend every meeting.

For example, the regular education teacher who is a member of the IEP team must participate in discussions and decisions about how to modify the general curriculum in the regular classroom to ensure the child's involvement and progress in the general curriculum and participation in the regular education environment.

Depending upon the specific circumstances, however, it may not be necessary for the regular education teacher to participate in discussions and decisions regarding, for example, the physical therapy needs of the child, if the teacher is not responsible for implementing that portion of the child's IEP.

In determining the extent of the regular education teacher's participation at IEP meetings, public agencies and parents should discuss and try to reach agreement on whether the child's regular education teacher that is a member of the IEP team should be present at a particular IEP meeting and, if so, for what period of time. The extent to which it would be appropriate for the regular education teacher member of the IEP team to participate in IEP meetings must be decided on a case-by-case basis.

25. If a child with a disability attends several regular classes, must all of the child's regular education teachers be members of the child's IEP team?

No. The IEP team need not include more than one regular education teacher of the child. If the participation of more than one regular education teacher would be beneficial to the child's success in school (e.g., in terms of enhancing the child's participation in the general curriculum), it would be appropriate for them to attend the meeting.

26. How should a public agency determine which regular education teacher and special education

teacher will be members of the IEP team for a particular child with a disability?

The regular education teacher who serves as a member of a child's IEP team should be a teacher who is, or may be, responsible for implementing a portion of the IEP, so that the teacher can participate in discussions about how best to teach the child.

If the child has more than one regular education teacher responsible for carrying out a portion of the IEP, the LEA may designate which teacher or teachers will serve as IEP team member(s), taking into account the best interest of the child.

In a situation in which not all of the child's regular education teachers are members of [FR Page 12478] the child's IEP team, the LEA is strongly encouraged to seek input from the teachers who will not be attending. In addition, (consistent with Sec. 300.342(b)), the LEA must ensure that each regular education teacher (as well as each special education teacher, related services provider, and other service provider) of an eligible child under this part (1) has access to the child's IEP, and (2) is informed of his or her specific responsibilities related to implementing the IEP, and of the specific accommodations, modifications and supports that must be provided to the child in accordance with the IEP.

In the case of a child whose behavior impedes the learning of the child or others, the LEA is encouraged to have a regular education teacher or other person knowledgeable about positive behavior strategies at the IEP meeting. This is especially important if the regular education teacher is expected to carry out portions of the IEP.

Similarly, the special education teacher or provider of the child who is a member of the child's IEP team should be the person who is, or will be, responsible for implementing the IEP. If, for example, the child's disability is a speech impairment, the special education teacher on the IEP team could be the speech-language pathologist.

27. For a child whose primary disability is a speech impairment, may a public agency meet its responsibility under Sec. 300.344(a)(3) to ensure that the IEP team includes ``at least one special education teacher, or, if appropriate, at least one special education provider of the child'' by including a speech-language pathologist on the IEP team?

> Yes, if speech is considered special education under State standards. As with other children with disabilities, the IEP team must also include at least one of the child's regular education teachers if the child is, or may be, participating in the regular education environment.

28. Do parents and public agencies have the option of inviting any individual of their choice be participants on their child's IEP team?

> The IEP team may, at the discretion of the parent or the agency, include ``other individuals who have knowledge or special expertise regarding the child * * *'' (Sec. 300.344(a) (6), italics added). Under Sec. 300.344(a)(6), these individuals are members of the IEP team. This is a change from prior law, which provided, without qualification, that parents or agencies could have other individuals as members of the IEP team at the discretion of the parents or agency.
>
> Under Sec. 300.344(c), the determination as to whether an individual has knowledge or special expertise, within the meaning of Sec. 300.344(a)(6), shall be made by the parent or public agency who has invited the individual to be a member of the IEP team.
>
> Part B does not provide for including individuals such as representatives of teacher organizations as part of an IEP team, unless they are included because of knowledge or special expertise regarding the child. (Because a representative of a teacher organization would generally be concerned

with the interests of the teacher rather than the interests of the child, and generally would not possess knowledge or expertise regarding the child, it generally would be inappropriate for such an official to be a member of the IEP team or to otherwise participate in an IEP meeting.)

29. Can parents or public agencies bring their attorneys to IEP meetings, and, if so under what circumstances? Are attorney's fees available for parents' attorneys if the parents are prevailing parties in actions or proceedings brought under Part B?

Section 300.344(a)(6) authorizes the addition to the IEP team of other individuals at the discretion of the parent or the public agency only if those other individuals have knowledge or special expertise regarding the child. The determination of whether an attorney possesses knowledge or special expertise regarding the child would have to be made on a case-by-case basis by the parent or public agency inviting the attorney to be a member of the team.

The presence of the agency's attorney could contribute to a potentially adversarial atmosphere at the meeting. The same is true with regard to the presence of an attorney accompanying the parents at the IEP meeting. Even if the attorney possessed knowledge or special expertise regarding the child (Sec. 300.344(a)(6)), an attorney's presence would have the potential for creating an adversarial atmosphere that would not necessarily be in the best interests of the child.

Therefore, the attendance of attorneys at IEP meetings should be strongly discouraged. Further, as specified in Section 615(i)(3)(D)(ii) of the Act and Sec. 300.513(c)(2)(ii), Attorneys' fees may not be awarded relating to any meeting of the IEP team unless the meeting is convened as a result of an administrative proceeding or judicial action, or, at the discretion of the State, for a mediation conducted prior to the request for a due process hearing.

30. Must related services personnel attend IEP meetings?

Although Part B does not expressly require that the IEP team include related services personnel as part of the IEP team (Sec. 300.344(a)), it is appropriate for those persons to be included if a particular related service is to be discussed as part of the IEP meeting. Section 300.344(a)(6) provides that the IEP team also includes ``at the discretion of the parent or the agency, other individuals who have knowledge or special expertise regarding the child, including related services personnel as appropriate. * * *'' (Italics added.)

Further, Sec. 300.344(a)(3) requires that the IEP team for each child with a disability include ``at least one special education teacher, or, if appropriate, at least one special education provider of the child * * *'' This requirement can be met by the participation of either (1) a special education teacher of the child, or (2) another special education provider such as a speech-language pathologist, physical or occupational therapist, etc., if the related service consists of specially designed instruction and is considered special education under the applicable State standard.

If a child with a disability has an identified need for related services, it would be appropriate for the related services personnel to attend the meeting or otherwise be involved in developing the IEP. As explained in the Committee Reports on the IDEA Amendments of 1997, ``Related services personnel should be included on the team when a particular related service will be discussed at the request of the child's parents or the school.'' (H. Rep. No. 105-95, p. 103 (1997); S. Rep. No. 105-17, p. 23 (1997)).

For example, if the child's evaluation indicates the need for a specific related service (e.g., physical therapy, occupational therapy, special transportation services, school social work services, school health services, or counseling), the agency should ensure that a qualified provider of that service either (1) attends the IEP meeting, or (2) provides a written recommendation concerning the nature, frequency, and amount of service to be provided to the child. This written recommendation could be a part of the evaluation report.

A public agency must ensure that all individuals who are necessary to develop an IEP that will meet the child's unique needs, and ensure the provision of FAPE to the child, participate in the child's IEP meeting.

31. Must the public agency ensure that all services specified in a child's IEP are provided?

Yes. The public agency must ensure that all services set forth in the child's IEP are provided, consistent with the child's needs as identified in the IEP. The agency may provide each of those services directly, through its own staff resources; indirectly, by contracting with another public or private agency; or through other arrangements.

In providing the services, the agency may use whatever State, local, Federal, and private sources of support are available for those purposes (see Sec. 300.301(a)); but the services must be at no cost to the parents, and the public agency remains responsible for ensuring that the IEP services are provided in a manner that appropriately meets the student's needs as specified in the IEP.

The SEA and responsible public agency may not allow the failure of another agency to provide service(s) described in the child's IEP to deny or delay the provision of FAPE to the child. (See Sec. 300.142, Methods of ensuring services.)

32. Is it permissible for an agency to have the IEP completed before the IEP meeting begins?

No. Agency staff may come to an IEP meeting prepared with evaluation findings and proposed recommendations regarding IEP content, but the agency must make it clear to the parents at the outset of the meeting that the services proposed by the agency are only recommendations for review and discussion with the parents.

Parents have the right to bring questions, concerns, and

recommendations to an IEP meeting as part of a full discussion, of the child's needs and the services to be provided to meet those needs before the IEP is finalized.

Public agencies must ensure that, if agency personnel bring drafts of some or all of the IEP content to the IEP meeting, there is a full discussion with the child's parents, before [FR Page 12479] the child's IEP is finalized, regarding drafted content and the child's needs and the services to be provided to meet those needs.

33. Must a public agency include transportation in a child's IEP as a related service?

As with other related services, a public agency must provide transportation as a related service if it is required to assist the disabled child to benefit from special education. (This includes transporting a preschool-aged child to the site at which the public agency provides special education and related services to the child, if that site is different from the site at which the child receives other preschool or day care services.)

In determining whether to include transportation in a child's IEP, and whether the child needs to receive transportation as a related service, it would be appropriate to have at the IEP meeting a person with expertise in that area. In making this determination, the IEP team must consider how the child's disability affects the child's need for transportation, including determining whether the child's disability prevents the child from using the same transportation provided to nondisabled children, or from getting to school in the same manner as nondisabled children.

The public agency must ensure that any transportation service included in a child's IEP as a related service is provided at public expense and at no cost to the parents, and that the child's IEP describes the transportation arrangement.

Even if a child's IEP team determines that the child does not require transportation as a related service, Section 504 of the Rehabilitation Act of 1973, as amended, requires that the child receive the same transportation provided to non-disabled children. If a public agency transports nondisabled children, it must transport disabled children under the same terms and conditions.

However, if a child's IEP team determines that the child does not need transportation as a related service, and the public agency transports only those children whose IEPs specify transportation as a related service, and does not transport nondisabled children, the public agency would not be required to provide transportation to a disabled child.

It should be assumed that most children with disabilities receive the same transportation services as nondisabled children. For some children with disabilities, integrated transportation may be achieved by providing needed accommodations such as lifts and other equipment adaptations on regular school transportation vehicles.

34. Must a public agency provide related services that are required to assist a child with a disability to benefit from special education, whether or not those services are included in the list of related services in Sec. 300.24?

The list of related services is not exhaustive and may include other developmental, corrective, or supportive services if they are required to assist a child with a disability to benefit from special education. This could, depending upon the unique needs of a child, include such services as nutritional services or service coordination.

These determinations must be made on an individual basis by each child's IEP team.

35. Must the IEP specify the amount of services or may it simply list the services to be provided?

The amount of services to be provided must be stated in the IEP, so that the level of the agency's commitment of resources will be clear to parents and other IEP team members

(Sec. 300.347(a)(6)). The amount of time to be committed to each of the various services to be provided must be (1) appropriate to the specific service, and (2) stated in the IEP in a manner that is clear to all who are involved in both the development and implementation of the IEP.

The amount of a special education or related service to be provided to a child may be stated in the IEP as a range (e.g., speech therapy to be provided three times per week for 30-45 minutes per session) only if the IEP team determines that stating the amount of services as a range is necessary to meet the unique needs of the child. For example, it would be appropriate for the IEP to specify, based upon the IEP team's determination of the student's unique needs, that particular services are needed only under specific circumstances, such as the occurrence of a seizure or of a particular behavior. A range may not be used because of personnel shortages or uncertainty regarding the availability of staff.

36. Under what circumstances is a public agency required to permit a child with a disability to use a school-purchased assistive technology device in the child's home or in another setting?

Each child's IEP team must consider the child's need for assistive technology (AT) in the development of the child's IEP (Sec. 300.346(a)(2)(v)); and the nature and extent of the AT devices and services to be provided to the child must be reflected in the child's IEP (Sec. 300.346(c)).

A public agency must permit a child to use school-purchased assistive technology devices at home or in other settings, if the IEP team determines that the child needs access to those devices in nonschool settings in order to receive FAPE (to complete homework, for example).

Any assistive technology devices that are necessary to ensure FAPE must be provided at no cost to the parents, and the parents cannot be charged for normal use, wear and tear. However, while ownership of the devices in these circumstances would remain with the public agency, State law, rather than Part B, generally would govern whether parents are liable for loss, theft, or damage due to negligence or misuse of publicly owned equipment used at home or in other settings in accordance with a child's IEP.

37. IEP Team Also Direct Placement. Can the IEP team also function as the group making the placement decision for a child with a disability?

Yes, a public agency may use the IEP team to make the placement decision for a child, so long as the group making the placement decision meets the requirements of Secs. 300.552 and 300.501(c), which requires that the placement decision be made by a group of persons, including the parents, and other persons knowledgeable about the child, the meaning of the evaluation data, and the placement options.

38. Punishment For Behavior For Disability. If a child's IEP includes behavioral strategies to address a particular behavior, can a child ever be suspended for engaging in that behavior?

If a child's behavior impedes his or her learning or that of others, the IEP team, in developing the child's IEP, must consider, if appropriate, development of strategies, including positive behavioral interventions, strategies and supports to address that behavior, consistent with Sec. 300.346(a)(2)(i).

This means that in most cases in which a child's behavior that impedes his or her learning or that of others is, or can be readily anticipated to be, repetitive, proper development of the child's IEP will include the development of strategies, including positive behavioral interventions, strategies and supports to address that behavior. See Sec. 300.346(c). This includes behavior that could violate a school code of conduct. A failure to, if appropriate, consider and address these behaviors in developing and implementing the child's IEP would constitute a denial of FAPE to the child.

Of course, in appropriate circumstances, the IEP team, which includes the child's parents, might determine that the child's behavioral intervention plan includes specific regular or alternative disciplinary measures, such as denial of certain privileges or short suspensions, that would result from particular infractions of school rules, along with positive behavior intervention strategies and supports, as a part of a comprehensive plan to address the child's behavior. Of course, if short suspensions that are included in a child's IEP are being implemented in a manner that denies the child access to the ability to progress in the educational program, the child would be denied FAPE.

Whether other disciplinary measures, including suspension, are ever appropriate for behavior that is addressed in a child's IEP will have to be determined on a case by case basis in light of the particular circumstances of that incident. However, school personnel may not use their ability to suspend a child for 10 days or less at a time on multiple occasions in a school year as a means of avoiding appropriately considering and addressing the child's behavior as a part of providing FAPE to the child.

39. Placement When Affecting Other Children. If a child's behavior in the regular classroom, even with appropriate interventions, would significantly impair the learning of others, can the group that makes the placement decision determine that placement in the regular classroom is inappropriate for that child?

The IEP team, in developing the IEP, is required to consider, when appropriate, strategies, including positive behavioral interventions, strategies and supports to address the behavior of a child with a disability whose behavior impedes his or her learning or that of others. If the IEP team determines that such supports, strategies or interventions are necessary to address the behavior of the child, those services must be included in the child's IEP. These provisions are designed to foster increased participation of children with disabilities in regular [FR Page 12480] education environments or other less restrictive environments, not to serve as a basis for placing children with disabilities in more restrictive settings.

The determination of appropriate placement for a child whose behavior is interfering with the education of others requires careful consideration of whether the child can appropriately function in the regular classroom if provided appropriate behavioral supports, strategies and interventions. If the child can appropriately function in the regular classroom with appropriate behavioral supports, strategies or interventions, placement in a more restrictive environment would be inconsistent with the least restrictive environment provisions of the IDEA. If the child's behavior in the regular classroom, even with the provision of appropriate behavioral supports, strategies or interventions, would significantly impair the learning of others, that placement would not meet his or her needs and would not be appropriate for that child.

40. Removal For Misconduct. May school personnel during a school year implement more than one short-term removal of a child with disabilities from his or her classroom or school for misconduct?

Yes. Under Sec. 300.520(a)(1), school personnel may order removal of a child with a disability from the child's current placement for not more than 10 consecutive school days for any violation of school rules, and additional removals of not more than 10 consecutive school days in that same school year for separate incidents of misconduct, as long as these removals do not constitute a change of placement under Sec. 300.519(b).

However, these removals are permitted only to the extent they are consistent with discipline that is applied to children without disabilities. Also, school personnel should be aware of constitutional due process protections that apply to suspensions of all children. *Goss v. Lopez*, 419 U.S. 565 (1975). Section 300.121(d) addresses the extent of the obligation to provide services after a child with a disability has been removed from his or her current placement for more than 10 school days in the same school year. [FR Page 12506]

PART III

SELECTED IDEA COURT CASES

CHAPTER EIGHT

COURT CASE OF PARENTS FORCING SCHOOL DISTRICT TO PAY FOR CHILD TO ATTEND PRIVATE SCHOOL

Union School Dist. v. Smith
15 F.3d 1519 (9th Cir. 1994)

**[Historical case showing the evolution
of the law. Courts may not uphold this ruling]**

Facts of Case

[Bernard Smith was a pupil in the Union School District (which for simplicity merely is called the "District"). At the District's 1989 IEP meeting, the Smiths showed (but did not give) the District part of a doctors report with diagnosing Bernard with autism. The District verbally offered to place Bernard at a facility called McKinnon, but when the parents replied negatively, they did not give the Smiths a formal, written placement offer. The Smith pulled their son out of the San Jose school and put him in a private school for autistic children in Los Angeles, then sued the District asking that they pay for that private schooling.

The Individuals With Disabilities Education Act is commonly known by its initials, "IDEA." This federal legislation is found in the codes beginning with 20 U.S.C. §1400. This statute guarantees and mandates that every handicapped child receives a "free" and" appropriate" public education.

There were many issues to be decided by the court, and only selected portions of the Circuit Judge Ferguson's court's decision are included below. The judge's decision is identifiable because it is significantly indented. Additionally, all citations and notations of missing text have been omitted to make the reading easier. Paragraphs are written by the author are in italics.

Court Ruling

> ***Information Withheld by Parents***. *The parents did not give the District a copy of the doctor's report, but merely showed them a portion of it indicating a diagnosis of autism. The school district did not, itself, make a diagnosis of autism. The issue is if the parents' failure to give the school a copy of the report or the District's lack of its own diagnosis offers the District a way to avoid paying for Bernard's private schooling?*

> > "Furthermore, the District was legally obligated to procure its own report from a specialist such as Dr. Siegel [who was the parent's physician]. The District must make "a full and individual evaluation of the child's educational needs," 34 C.F.R. § 300.531, and must "ensure ... [that the] evaluation [of the student] is made by a multidisciplinary team ... including at least one teacher or other specialists with knowledge in the area of suspected disability" (i.e., a specialist in autism). 34 C.F.R. §300.532(e). Any failure of the Smiths to turn over portions of a specialist's report cannot excuse the District's failure to procure the same information for itself.

The District contends that McKinnon, the District's program for autistic children, was an appropriate placement for Bernard. As the district court found, and the District concedes, the District never formally offered Bernard a placement at McKinnon. The District argues that it did not offer McKinnon because the Smiths expressed their unwillingness to consider it as a placement. Thus, the question we face is whether the District was required to make a formal offer under the IDEA.

We find that a school district cannot escape its obligation under the IDEA to offer formally an appropriate educational placement by arguing that a disabled child's parents expressed unwillingness to accept that placement. The IDEA explicitly requires written prior notice to parents when an educational agency proposes, or refuses, to initiate or change the educational placement of a disabled child."

Must IDEA Be Followed Exactly? *If the basic concept of the IDEA is followed, does it matter if the EXACT procedure is not followed? For example, if the parents state they do not want their child placed at a certain facility, isn't it just form over substance to require a school district to provide written notification that will be rejected?*

"The Supreme Court has explained the great importance of [following] such procedural components of the IDEA. We find that this formal requirement has an important purpose that is not merely technical, and we therefore believe it should be enforced rigorously.

The requirement of a formal, written offer creates a clear record that will do much to eliminate troublesome factual disputes many years later about when placements were offered, what placements were offered, and what additional educational assistance was offered to supplement a placement, if any. Furthermore, a formal, specific offer from a school district will greatly assist parents in "presenting] complaints with respect to any matter relating to the educational placement of the child.

For example, in this case, a formal offer of McKinnon would have served several purposes. It would have alerted the Smiths to the need to consider seriously whether McKinnon was an appropriate placement under the IDEA. The Smiths could not have been reimbursed for their unilateral placement of Bernard at the Clinic if McKinnon were an appropriate placement. Also, if a formal offer were made, the Smiths could have decided whether to oppose McKinnon or to accept it with the supplement of additional education services."

Appropriate Not Best Education. *If there are two school opportunities, and one is more expensive or somehow better for that child, must the school district pay for the one that offers the best education for that child?*

"An 'appropriate' public education does not mean the absolutely best or 'potential maximizing' education for the individual child. The states are obliged to provide 'a basic floor of opportunity' through a program 'individually designed to provide educational benefit to the handicapped child.'

If a parent believes that a school district has failed to offer a free appropriate public education, parents may place an eligible child in an appropriate private program. Parents have an equitable right to reimbursement for the cost of providing an appropriate private education when a school district has failed to offer a child a free appropriate public education."

What is Appropriate. *For Bernard's needs, would a Com-*
municatively Handicapped Class at a school called "Carlton" be an
"appropriate" education for his handicap?

> "During this period, the District's sole explicit offer
> (as set forth in its November 1 letter) was an educa-
> tional program implementing Bernard's IEP through
> seventeen and one-half hours a week in the Com-
> municatively Handicapped Class at Carlton School,
> supplemented by some one-to-one behavior modifi-
> cation counseling.
>
> The Hearing Officer found that this program was in-
> appropriate. The Hearing Officer found that there
> were no other autistic children at Carlton and there
> was no evidence that the teacher had been trained to
> work with autistic children. Furthermore, the Hear-
> ing Officer heeded the testimony of the witnesses
> who had extensive experience with autistic children,
> who testified that the learning environment at Carl-
> ton was inappropriate for Bernard's individual needs.
> [He found that] Bernard requires a more restrictive
> and less stimulating environment than that offered at
> Carlton. He requires full-time, one-to-one instruc-
> tion and is unable to benefit from group instruction.
>
> In light of the deference we grant the Hearing Officer
> as to judgments of educational policy, we find that
> Bernard's placement at Carlton was inappropriate
> because it was insufficiently individually designed to
> meet Bernard's special needs."

[If the District had an appropriate program, even if it were
outside the normal school district, the parents would have had
to accept that class. Even if such a class was not offered by the
District, parents could not just pick the school or institution they
want. It must usually be made in conjunction with input from
the District.

This case is <u>somewhat unique</u>, because the District thought *that because Bernard was in Los Angeles, Bernard ceased to become a student of their district. Unfortunately, it was an expensive mistake by the District.]*

Receive Fees for Education. *Since the Court found that the District did not offer an "appropriate" education, must it pay for Bernard's school that the parents have chosen? Must it pay even though the school district Bernard attended was in San Jose and the private school his parents placed him in was in Los Angeles?*

"The Supreme Court has held that a court may order a school district to reimburse parents who have unilaterally placed their child in an appropriate private special education after the school district has failed to offer an appropriate public education. The Smiths are entitled to reimbursement for tuition at the Clinic because the District failed to offer them an appropriate placement and the Smith's placement of Bernard at the Clinic was appropriate."

Receive Free Lodging, Airfare, and Transportation. *Since the private school was hundreds of miles away, must the District also pay for Bernard's housing, meals, transportation to school and airfare between San Jose and Los Angeles?*

The Hearing Officer and the district court also found that the Smiths were entitled to reimbursement for transportation costs to and from the Clinic each day, the transportation costs of commuting between San Jose and Los Angeles at the beginning and end of Bernard's participation in the program and when the school is officially closed to students (i.e., Thanksgiving, winter and spring breaks), and to reimbursement for the cost of lodging for Bernard and Mrs. Smith in Los Angeles.

"Under IDEA, a 'free appropriate public education' includes not only special education, but also 'related services.' Related services include 'transportation,.. and other supportive services ... as may be required to assist a child with a disability to benefit from special education.' 20 U.S.C. 1401(a)(17). If a child's appropriate special education placement is at a non-residential program not within daily commuting distance of the family residence, transportation costs and lodging near the school are related services that are required to assist that child to benefit from the special education."

**Lesson from this case
and cases like it**

Don't take the IEP lightly or assume it doesn't matter. The IEP and the placement of handicapped children may be one of the most important aspects of your educational requirements. Learn the procedures, and if in doubt, call your IEP specialists or special education officer for assistance. While a court today may not reach exactly the same result, the concept of having to adhere precisely to the existing requirements of the IEP is very relevant today.]

CHAPTER NINE

TEACHER WINS $1 MILLION WHEN FIRED BY SCHOOL DISTRICT FOR ADVOCATING FOR DISABLED STUDENTS

Settlegoode v. Portland Public Schools
371 F.3d 503 (9th Cir. 2004)

Facts of Case

Dr. Pamella Settlegoode was hired by Portland Public Schools as an Adapted Physical Education teacher for the 1998-99 academic year on a probationary basis. Her job included teaching the disabled students as well as drafting individualized education programs (IEP) for them. Settlegoode soon became concerned about the way disabled students were treated in the Portland schools. She had trouble finding a place to teach her high school students; material and equipment were often lacking, inadequate or unsafe.

Settlegoode tried to talk to her immediate supervisor, Susan Winthrop, about these problems. Winthrop told Settlegoode that she was the only one who had ever complained about the facilities for disabled students. [She then wrote a

letter to the head of special education and later to the super-
intendent expressing her concern.]

During Settlegoode's first year of teaching, her performance evaluations were generally positive. Winthrop's evaluations [of Settlegoode after her] letters, were much more
negative. The evaluation ended by stating that, "[i]f Dr. Settlegoode's work continues at its present quality, renewal of
contract for another year cannot be recommended."

[Her contract to teach was not renewed, so Settlegoode
sued the school district and her supervisor for violation of
§504 for not protecting disabled students, her right to free
speech, and violation of Oregon's Whistleblower Act. Since
IEPs were involved, the §504 retaliatory issues should be
equally applicable to the ADA. The jury awarded Settlegoode $1 million in damages, and the judge overturned the
jury award. Settlegoode appealed to the federal Court of
Appeals, which reinstated her $1 million judgment. Inter-
esting, but not relevant, according to one website the school
district's attorneys' fee was over one-half million dollars.]

Court Decision

If the School Violated Settlegoode's Free-
dom of Speech. When a government employee alleges
that he has been punished in retaliation for exercising his
First Amendment rights, we engage in a three-part inquiry:
To prevail, an employee must prove (1) that the conduct at
issue is constitutionally protected, and (2) that it was a substantial or motivating factor in the punishment. Even if the
employee discharges that burden, (3) the government can escape liability by showing that it would have taken the same
action even in the absence of the protected conduct. The
magistrate judge found that Settlegoode "presented substantial evidence that the content of her speech reporting
violations of the law by the District was a factor ... for the
non-renewal decision."

Even if defendants had shown that Settlegoode's IEPs
were inadequate [which the evidence does not show], that

stil. would not have been enough. Defendants were required to show that they "would have taken the same action even in the absence of the protected conduct." Proof that Settlegoode's IEPs were deficient [which the evidence does not conclusively show] only tells us that the school district could have chosen not to renew Settlegoode's contract for reasons independent of the protected conduct. The magistrate judge said almost nothing about this distinction, but it is a crucial one.

Defendants, for example, offered no evidence that other teachers had been fired for drafting inadequate IEPs in the past or that it was unusual for new teachers to struggle with IEP writing. To the contrary, two teachers in Settlegoode's department testified that drafting IEPs is difficult, that it is easy to criticize any IEP and that IEPs would be a good place "to create a paper trail." As the burden is on the defendant [school district] to show Settlegoode's contract would not have been renewed, even if she had kept silent, we cannot agree with the magistrate judge [and support and reinstate the jury award of $1 million].

If the School Personnel Had Government Immunity. [Since Settlegoode's First Amendment rights of Freedom of Speech were violated, the next question the court faced was if the school's personnel were immune from liability for violating Settlegoode's rights.]

Public officials are immune from liability "insofar as their conduct does not violate clearly established statutory or constitutional rights of which a reasonable person would have known." Where plaintiff is a government employee claiming violations of his First Amendment rights, he must show that two things were clearly established: (1) that his speech involved a matter of public concern, and (2) that the interests served by allowing him to express himself outweighed the state's interest in promoting workplace efficiency and avoiding workplace disruption.

When balancing interests under the second prong of the test, defendants must show "actual injury to . . . legitimate interests' beyond the 'disruption that necessarily accompanies such speech." The magistrate judge found that "plaintiff's speech [was] within the ambit of the First Amendment," and thus was a matter of public concern.

The jury here was properly instructed that, "[b]ecause some anger or unhappiness necessarily accompanies speech on issues of public concern, Defendants must prove that the School District suffered an actual injury to its legitimate interests beyond mere disruption of the workplace." The jury's verdict in favor of Settlegoode necessarily reflected a finding that any disruption her comments might have aroused was outweighed by Settlegoode's interest in free expression.

There was a strong interest in allowing Settlegoode to express herself. Not only were Settlegoode's core First Amendment rights implicated, but her speech may have had important effects for the disabled students in the district and their parents. Teachers are uniquely situated to know whether students are receiving the type of attention and education that they deserve and, in this case, are federally entitled to.

We have long recognized "the importance of allowing teachers to speak out on school matters," because "[t]eachers are, as a class, the members of a community most likely to have informed and definite opinions" on such matters. This is particularly so with respect to disabled children, who may not be able to communicate effectively that they lack appropriate facilities.

Teachers may, therefore, be the only guardians of these children's rights and interests during the school day. Whether or not Settlegoode's assertions were accurate, or were communicated in the best manner possible, it is clear that the subject matter of her expression was of public importance. The administrators who testified also failed to show that Settlegoode's letter was unusually disruptive or caused actual injury.

Lessons from This Case

Was the lawsuit necessary? Settlegoode was unable to find another job after she was fired. While it is hard to know exactly what influence her letters and firing had, it is probable that anyone who sent out over 50 letters and was not able to land any employment was blackballed by her supervisors. The author suspects after Settlegoode found she could not be re-employed elsewhere she finally turned to the courts. The emotional toll from lawsuits can be exhausting if not painful and should be considered carefully before proceeding.

If special education teachers face pressure or disciplinary action for advocating for their disabled students this case may help. One of the primary reasons for including this case in the book is the belief by the author that merely mentioning this case (and some of the wording of the court decision) is enough to scare most school districts. It may forestall any negative action on their part especially in states like California and Oregon that are part of the 9th federal district.

How important were Settlegoode's letters?

It is the author's opinion that without the "paper trail" the letters provided, the trial might have been a situation of "he said, she said" where the jury might not believe Settlegoode even complained or that the school district was punitive and dismissive in their reactions. Of course, it didn't hurt that Settlegoode was married to an attorney well versed in civil rights litigation and who could emphasize the need to provide a well-documented paper trail. Settlegoode had letters, calendars with written notes of what happened on what dates, and lengthy notes made for her file.

During trial an attorney can hold up a letter from a special education teacher in front of a school administrator and ask questions. For example, on paragraph two of the letter the attorney might ask: do you recognize the letter; how did you react to paragraph two; do you believe if true paragraph two states violations of federal law; were any of the facts of paragraph two true; did you personally investigate any of the allegations of paragraph two; what does federal law state about meeting the needs of §504 students [or an IEP]; and similar type questions for each paragraph.

If you as a special education teacher or as a parent are going to fight with a school district it is important to have a paper trail. If you are really in a fight, it is the author's opinion to write the letters in a way that you would feel satisfied if they were read in front of a jury.

If you are a parent, it may be that if you show the Pamella Settlegoode case to a sympathetic special education teacher, they may feel safer complaining to their school district. It may make them feel comfortable enough to advocate for your child over and above what they would normally do.

Why Couldn't School Fire a Probationary Teacher?

It is interesting to note that Settlegoode was a probationary teacher, meaning she was not covered by any union contract. She could be fired for almost any reason except one in violation of the law. Just as it is illegal to discriminate on the basis of race, color or creed, so too is it illegal to be fired for properly advising the school district to follow federal law.

CHAPTER TEN

COURT CASE OF PARENTS REFUSING TO AGREE TO THE RECOMMENDED IEP PLACEMENT

**Bd. of Educ. of S.D. 21 v. Ill. St. Bd. of Educ.
933 F.2d 712 (7th Cir. 1991)**

The 2004 reauthorization of IDEA solved this issue and provided a mechanism for going forward when the parent obstructs or refuses to participate. Still, the case shows how the law evolved (an issue at a time), and provides sound reasoning on how future courts may read statutory provisions.

Facts of Case

Adam Brozer was a junior high school student in Buffalo Grove, Illinois, who was diagnosed with a behavior disorder and learning disability. During the 1989 school year, his behavior became more and more disruptive and even violent at times. Further, educationally, Adam was doing poorly at school. At Adam's second IEP meeting the school district wanted to move Adam to an alternative public school (the

BEC/Jack London School), which specialized in children with severe behavior disorders.

The Brozers refused to approve this placement and demanded that Adam be placed in the special education class in a Holmes, Illinois junior high school. The school district reluctantly agreed. At the Holmes school, Adam did poorly academically, and behaviorally he was totally out of control.

To complicate matters, the Brozers refused to allow the district to discipline Adam. They refused to allow detention or quiet lunches as interventional strategies, and they also denigrated the school in front of Adam.

In November 1989 the district held its third IEP, and it was found the current situation was not meeting Adam's educational needs. The district again recommended Adam be placed at the BEC/Jack London School. The parents still refused consent.

There were many issues decided by the court, and only selected portions of Circuit Judge Flaum's judicial decision are reported below. The judge's decision is easily identified because it is the significantly intended text. Paragraphs written by the author are in italics. Additionally, all citations are left out, and notations indicating missing text have been omitted to make the reading easier.

Court Ruling

What if the Parents Don't Agree to the Placement. *The statutes provide a procedure if the parents refuse to consent to an initial IEP evaluation. 20 USC §1414(a)(1)(C)(ii). However, here the issue is what if the parents consent to the evaluation, but disagree with the placement and refuse the consent to the placement. What can the district do?*

> "When Adam's parents refused to consent to this placement [at the BEC/Jack London School] the district initiated the informal due process review procedure to determine the appropriate placement for

Adam. [The procedure is found at 20 USC §1415(b) (1)(E) requires a Level 1 hearing, and if appealed, then a Level 2 hearing, which can, itself, be appealed to a federal district court.]

[At the Level 1 hearing] the Level I hearing officer agreed with the district that Adam was primarily behavior disordered and only secondarily learning disabled. The hearing officer also noted the "irreconcilable differences" that had developed between the Brozers and the district [and the Brozers' efforts to continuously undercut the school district's efforts]. In light of these problems, the Level I hearing officer found that Adam's education could only 'be effectuated if the parents are not involved on a continuous basis in second-guessing the disciplinary efforts of the educators.' To this end Level I hearing officer ordered that Adam be enrolled at public expense at a private residential ['live in'] school.

The Brozers appealed the Level I decision. The Level II officer, like the Level I officer, noted the extremely adversarial relationship between the Brozers and the district, likening the Brozers' mindset to a "siege mentality." He agreed that 'the state of mind of the parents was likely to affect the success or failure of the district's proposed placement at Jack London School.' In fact, he stated that because the district's proposed placement had been 'poisoned' in Adam's mind by his parents, there was 'no reason to expect that the BEC/Jack London placement will be successful.' The Level II officer thus concurred in the district's judgment that Adam needed a more restrictive placement than Holmes.

However, he felt the Level I officer had not upheld her obligation to order the least restrictive placement [required under the statutes]. Specifically, he did not think that the evidence supported the Level I officer's finding that Adam needed to be enrolled at a private residential school. He ordered the school district to find Adam a placement at a private day school

[not a residential, live-in school. The school district appealed this decision to the federal district court and then ultimately this court, the federal Court of Appeals.]"

Must the district consider the parent's hostility to a placement? *The court found that ordinarily, Adam should attend a special education public school class. However, because the parents have so poisoned Adam against such a class, the court found it unlikely that such a class would be successful. Therefore, the court ordered placement in the private day school.*

The district argued it was unfair to make this evaluation based on the Brozers' antagonism to the public school placement. If the court made its decision based largely on the Brozers' attitude, it would in effect be rewarding the counter-productive attitude of the parents. One of the issues, therefore, was whether the placement can be made ignoring the parents' attitude, or if their antagonism must be included in deciding the proper placement.

"Adam [should] be placed in a private day school rather than at BEC/Jack London. Adam would not be able to satisfactorily obtain the required education benefits from the district's proposed placement in light of the history of Adam's and his parents' relationship with the district."

The school district argues that it was improper as a matter of law for the district court to consider the Brozers' hostility to the BEC/Jack London placement. This contention is incorrect.

The sole legal requirement is that the IEP be designed to serve the educational interests of the child. The EHA does not limit the factors that can be considered in judging the likely impact of the IEP on the child so long as they bear on the question of expected educational benefits.

In this case, the district court made a factual finding that the parents' attitudes were severe enough to doom any attempt to educate Adam at BEC/Jack

London. This finding had obvious and direct relevance to any assessment of the probable benefit to Adam of the BEC/Jack London placement.

The court only considered the Brozers' attitude to the extent that it related to the ultimate question of whether the court could deem the BEC/Jack London placement to be "reasonably calculated" to supply educational benefit to Adam.

Allowing a consideration of parental hostility to a state-proposed IEP to the extent that it limits the lEP's benefit to the child will result at times in the rejection of the school district's proposal simply because the parents, perhaps irrationally, oppose it.

The plaintiff school district here exhorts us not to adopt a position that will "reward" parents for aberrant or distasteful behavior. Under the EHA, however, our concern is not rewarding or punishing parents. The appropriate concern is finding a program which will be of educational benefit to the child. Were we to adopt the school district's position and hold that parental attitudes can never be considered even if they have impaired the workability of the IEP for the child, this would in effect be punishing children for the actions of their parents.

A child whose parents oppose an IEP so vehemently and vocally as to 'doom' its prospects should not be enrolled in the placement merely to enable educational agencies and federal courts to 'discipline' parents. The EHA makes clear whose interest must be paramount.

Can parents then decide placement?

If the district must consider objections of parent that are so strong as to affect the value of an IEP program, do parent's then have the right to merely object and decide where the child should go?

"Moreover, we do not share the school district's concern that under our ruling parents will be able to feign opposition to obtain their preferred placement. Our ruling does nothing to alter the ability of hearing officers to make credibility determinations. Hearing officers are best positioned to assess whether a family's hostility is manufactured or whether parental attitudes pose a real threat to the success of the proposed IEP.

Their findings are thus entitled to 'due weight' by a district court on appeal. Under the regime established by the EHA, the district courts also retain the ability to test the parents' sincerity if it remains a viable issue on appeal to federal court, for they are allowed to hear additional evidence at either party's request.

This Court is obligated to give any factual finding that emerges from this process deferential 'clear error' review, whether the district court finds that the parents' obstructionist attitude will have little real effect on the child's education or, as in this case, that the parents' hostility is so entrenched as to preclude hopes for the proposed IEP."

Lesson from this Case

Most of the time the school IEP team can encourage reluctant parents to "go along" with the IEP team's recommendations. Often the "let's try it and see what happens" approach will buy time and make it harder for parents to change their mind. If parents truly and violently object, then the IEP team must determine if that hostility will affect the child's performance and hence the child's placement.

Author's Note

Even though this was an Illinois case, and there was a dissenting opinion, and the author personally dislikes the result, this was the law. This was an appellate case interrupting federal law. (See 78 C.J.S. Schools And School Districts §716).

The author feels this case would be decided differently under the new IDEA reauthorization, but it shows the reasoning of the court and perhaps what to expect on other issues.

Court Case of Inadequately Written IEP That Violates Federal Law

Chris D. v. Montgomery County Bd. of Educ.
753 F.Supp. 922 (M.D. Ala. 1990)

Introduction

As important as this case is, the decision is also highly technical and detailed. Special education teachers are usually limited by time constraints and the IEP format selected by their
school district. Nevertheless, this case demonstrates what the
court require should the matter end in litigation. For parents
of special needs children, if your child's IEP does not mirror
what is required by this case, the school district may have
violated federal law.

Facts of Case

It was not until 1989, when Corry was a fifth-grade student
in the Montgomery, Alabama public schools that he was
given an IEP and specialized education. However, despite

the special education Corry received, he made a minimal educational improvement. Additionally, Corry suffered from emotional troubles that often made him a disruptive influence on the class.

One of the primary issues in the federal court case concerned the adequacy of the IEP, which was a preprinted form with generic fill-in-the-blank responses. Further, the question of the validity of Corry's IEP was questioned for appropriateness since Corry made little educational improvement.

The Decision

Essential Parts of an IEP. *Other chapters of this book list the code sections that describe what information must be in an Individual Education Plan ("IEP"). At the minimum, at least eight elements that must be included in an IEP:*

A. **Present Level of Educational Performance**. The IEP must describe the student's current level of educational performance. The courts have held that it is impossible to measure or set goals without ascertaining (in reasonably meaningful terms) the child's current educational status.

B. **Set Goals**. The IEP must set forth annual goals that are both measurable and realistic in furthering the child's educational development. Such goals may include benchmarks and short-term objectives for meeting both the child's disability and the child's other needs that result from that disability.

C. **Modifications and Related Services Needed**. The IEP needs to document what changes are needed in the educational environment, including special educational and related services.

D. **Degree of Inclusion.** The IEP should state to what extent the student is to be included in the general education settings (sometimes called "mainstreaming"). It needs to describe those activities and situations in which the child will participate in regular classrooms.

E. **Modifications in Standardized Tests**. If the state or school district has standardized tests it administers to its students, the IEP must indicate if the child will take those tests, and if so, what modifications are needed when administering the test. If the student will not take the standardized tests, then the IEP needs to identify how the student will be assessed.

F. **Timeline**. The IEP must include a beginning date for the modifications and the duration, frequency and location for those modifications.

G. **Transition Services for Older Children**. Once the child reaches age 16, there are set ages at which different transition services must be evaluated and included. These transition service will help the child adjust life after he or she leaves school.

H. **Method of Evaluating the Child's Progress**. The IEP must state how the child's progress in achieving the annual goals are to be measured and how the parents are to be informed of this progress.

Author's Note. In the author's opinion, much of the litigation concerning the legal adequacy of the IEP seems to center on three areas: (a) the description of the child's present level of performance, (b) the relevance of the goals that are set, and (c) the measurement of those goals. All areas of the IEP can, and probably have been litigated, but the next three major paragraph headings focus on different cases which have interrupted and stated the requirements for these three key areas.

Detailed Description of Child's Present Level of Performance. The child's current educational status must be detailed and sufficiently described so that a third party can ascertain the child's current development. With the concept that a picture is worth a thousand words, the example below is considered an excellent IEP. It is part of a vigorously attacked IEP that a federal court upheld and used to find for the school district. The child was hearing-impaired, suffered from multiple physical handicaps, and was unable to speak intelligibly.[1] [*The material below is from a different court case, which is why the student is named David.*]

> Approximately four pages of the IEP are devoted to David's then present level of academic performance. The IEP first describes efforts to measure David's intellectual ability by stating the scores of two IQ tests. The IEP then endeavors to describe David's general information level by detailing the results of two tests to measure educational achievement. The IEP goes on to describe what has been observed about David generally.

> For example, the IEP states that David's sign language level may be described as "expressive signs are telegraphic with some three word correct syntax. Intelligibility of signs by adults in speech class- 15%, in Lunch by supervisor-5%"

> Following the statement of David's general

---

1. *French v. Omaha Public Schools*, 766 F.Supp. 765 (D. Neb. 1991)

performance levels are specific statements concerning student David's 'communicative ability, language ability, reading ability, mathematics ability, science ability, social studies ability, occupational therapy situation, and physical therapy situation. Included in each of these categories is a description of David's performance which most often contains observations of David as well as his scores on various testing instruments.

For example, the IEP states that David has "manuscript and cursive writing skills," but his writing is "at slow speed," while his "letters are formed and produced correctly."

In the area of communication, the IEP endeavors to describe David's lip reading skills by referring to the "Craig Lipreading Inventory." In the area of language, the IEP describes both David's age equivalency to other students (5-6-year-old age) and his grade equivalency to other students (first to second grade equivalent, but at only the first percentile in terms of language competence). The IEP then proceeds to describe David's present language performance skills in terms of beginning knowledge, vocabulary, analogies, antonyms and synonyms, and concept development. Similar examples could be given for the IEP's presentation of David's reading ability, mathematical ability, science ability, social studies ability, occupational therapy needs, and physical therapy needs in terms of the IEP's effort to describe David's level of performance at that time.

[The actual section of the IEP relating to a description of David's communication skills are below.]

> Uses ASL signs in English word order.
> Rarely initiates communication (BTNI 2/89).
> Communication strategies based on shared knowledge and

has difficulty generalizing to other topics (experiences/maps) (BTNI 2/89).

Can request, answer, acknowledge (head nod) and describe functions present when at his vocabulary and language level (BTNI 2/89).

Has manuscript and cursive writing skills. Manuscript at slow speed. Cursive letters are formed and produced correctly.

Computer skills! Keyboarding skills-presently does not know locations of keys. Has good memory for development of keyboarding. Finger dexterity and motor movement creates limitations (ability statement to use computer at present).

Speech production skills are below 3-year level.

Responses limited to sign, written word, short phrase (BTNI 2/89).

Lipreading skills: Craig Lipreading Inventory 9/11/89

Picture matched to word – 50% correct

Sentence recognition – 1/6 correct—student did not attend to speaker for sentence)

Listening skills: Environmental awareness (DLM tapes) 6/10, 8/10, 5/6, 7/8, 2/5, 2/5 correct

Appropriate Goals Producing Results. *[Author's note. The material below is again from the student Corry in his court case.]* That is occasional argument, perhaps sometimes with justification, that teachers set the child's IEP goals intentionally low so that they can be assured of meeting their objectives. Whatever goals are set, they must be able to produce a reasonable improvement in the child's education, especially in the area of his deficiency. In this case Corry's IEP seemed to produce little actual improvement. The federal court was quick to criticize that IEP as severely inadequate.

Indeed, despite the constant, individual attention Corry has received from special education teachers, the results of a number of standardized tests administered to him in the last several years indicate that as of September 1990, he has made no substantial educational progress since 1987, before he began receiving special education. These test scores demonstrate that the instruction offered by the school board has done nothing to advance the principal purpose of providing special education to Corry, namely, to raise his abysmally low rate of learning.

The court cannot agree with the school board's argument that because Corry has learned something in the last several years, he is therefore receiving an educational benefit from special education. These test results indicate that he would be in the same position he is now if he had never received any special education. Indeed, children learn something over the course of time from simply existing and watching television, even if they never attend a day of school. Under the Act, an educational benefit is not conferred anytime a student is not left to vegetate. The court agrees that the EHA cannot be so trivialized. The Act requires a plan of instruction under which educational progress is likely. The Act requires a plan likely to produce progress, not retrogression or trivial educational advancement. Clearly, Congress did not intend that a school system could discharge its duty under the Act by providing a program that produces some minimal academic achievement, no matter how trivial.

Reliable Measurement Of The Goals. The goals that are set must be more than mere teacher observation. They must be objective and measurable by recognized tests that can analyze a child's deficits and his or her improvement. They must be such that an objective third party, such as a judge or other teacher can feel they accurately reflect a child's development in a way that has true meaning.

Preprinted Forms With Generic Language Inadequate. In this case, the school's IEP consisted primarily of a preprinted form of generic responses which the special education teacher filled in. The court was quick to dispose of that method as totally inadequate.

For example, the first objective, in Corry's new IEP, provided, in standard form: "The student will maintain a/an __% average in math on the 3rd grade level," with "80" written in the blank space, and stated that Corry would be evaluated by reference to his "Daily work" and "Chapter tests."

The IEP also provided that Corry would be "mainstreamed"-that he would attend regular classes in several subjects, including Health, Art, Physical Education, Music, and Social Studies. Finally, a supplement to the IEP also consisted of several pre-printed pages which listed various more specific-sounding "objectives" or "competencies," such as "The student will be able to: Identify periods to punctuate sentences with __% accuracy," with the figure "80" again written in. The supplement also indicated that Corry would be evaluated by means of "unit tests."

The academic objectives and methods of evaluation, found in Corry's most recent "Individualized Educational Program" are, like those included in previous IEPs, inadequate in at least two principal respects. First, it is obvious from the face of the documents comprising the IEP that it is not truly "individualized" -in other words, it is not tailored to Corry's particular needs and abilities. The IEP should describe "specially designed instruction" to be provided [to the] handicapped child. The IEP consists of several standard, pre-printed forms on which Corry's teacher from last year has merely filled in grade, levels, percentages, and textbook names.

Second, the January 1990, IEP "fails to specify strategies for adequately evaluating Corry's academic progress and determining which teaching methods are effective and which need to be revised.

Although the IEP repeatedly, incants the phrases, "daily work" and "unit tests," the routine practice of Corry's' teacher last year was to mark mistakes in his work allowing Corry to correct these errors before grading him, and also to divide each end-of-unit test into smaller sections which she assigned to Corry separately. The court was presented with convincing expert testimony that such techniques cannot accurately gauge what material Corry has actually learned, in the sense of what he has mastered and retained rather than what he has simply committed to short term memory. [The] IEP must include "evaluation procedures and schedules for determining ... whether instructional objectives are being achieved."

Can't Base Goals On Teacher's Subjective Opinions. Some school districts tried to avoid setting specific, measurable goals, relying on the teacher's evaluation. The thought was that since the teacher's measurements are not based on standardized or scientifically approved tests, the results can not be challenged. The courts were quick to find such methods inadequate and invalid. *[Author's note. In other cases, the court discussed these requirements in detail.[1] Portions of several cases have been pieced together to form this chapter thereby providing a more detailed and wider discussion of what needs to be in an IEP. This student below is named Frank.]*

The IEPs include only broad, generic objectives and vague, subjective methods for monitoring Frank's progress. For example, the first goal in Frank's IEP provided that he would be evaluated on the listed objectives by reference

---

1. *Bonadonna v. Cooperman*, 619 F.Supp. 975 (D. NJ 1985). In Evans vs. Bd. of Educ. of Rhienbeck Cent. Sch. Dist., 930 F. Supp. 83, 97 (S.D.N.Y. 1996)

to "teacher observation" and "80% accuracy." With reference to the second goal IEP provided that he would be evaluated on by "teacher observation" and "80% success." ... [The IEP] did not set forth measurable criteria to assess progress.

[For example, going back to the first case involving Corry, the court said:] the first objective, in Corrys new IEP, provided, in standard form: "The student will maintain a___/ an ___% average in math on the 3rd grade level," with "80" written in the blank space, and stated that Corry would be evaluated by reference to his "Daily work" and "Chapter tests."

Objectives Must Be Specific And Measurable.

In understanding how to write an IEP is probably easier to see what a federal court upheld as a good example of an IEP and one which withstood an aggressive attack by his guardian. The child was hearing-impaired, suffered from multiple physical handicaps, and was unable to speak intelligibly. Despite a very extensive and detailed IEP, the guardian attacked the IEP as insufficient. The court upheld the IEP and found for the district.[1]

Insofar as listing objectives, evaluation procedures, and schedules for determining achievement of educational objectives, the IEP is quite detailed. This section of the IEP is twenty-three pages long and lists approximately eighty objectives. There are objectives for art, computers, language, math, physical education, reading, pragmatics, science, social studies, auditory training, occupational therapy, and physical therapy.

---

1. *French v. Omaha Public Schools*, 766 F.Supp. 765 (D. Neb. 1991)

For each objective there is a description of the person who is to implement the objective, a narrative description of the objective, a statement of what evaluation procedures will used, and a schedule for when those evaluation procedures will be implemented. A few examples will serve to illustrate how the IEP approaches this area.

One of the objectives for language was the following:

> Objective for: language implemented by: classroom Teacher: Given reading a paragraph with three to ten specified events at second to third-grade reading level, student will retell the content of the story, using key vocabulary cue list without teacher assistance (independently) at 80% accuracy.

> Evaluation Procedure: Independently read paragraph and asked to retell story content of the ten events, given list of key vocabulary.

> Evaluation Schedule: Weekly.

As a further example, the IEP describes an objective for "pragmatics" this way:

> Objective for: pragmatics implemented by: speech/language pathologist. Student will demonstrate the ability to perform each of the following six language functions: requesting, discussion of effect, expression of need, initiation of communication, question asking, greetings, taking conversational turns, and describing. When given a direction or when asked a question by the speech pathologist in speech class, student will use the correct language function with no prompt using, voice and sign (finger-spelling) simultaneously at the 80% level on 9 of 10 occasions.

> Evaluation Procedure: Based on observation and charting by speech pathologist.

> Evaluation Schedule: Monthly

> Progress:

Response 1. Student will request clarification, actions and objects.

Response 2. Student will discuss his feelings using complete English sentences.

Response 3. Student will initiate a conversation with the speech pathologist, paraprofessional and lunchroom supervisor and take three conversational turns.

Response 4. Student will express his needs in speech class (example: "I am thirsty.")

Response 5. Student will initiate and respond directly to greetings by adults and peers at school.

Response 6. Student will describe an unknown object so that an adult can guess what it is.

Lesson From This Case

A good IEP takes considerable testing, meticulous detail, and much thought. It is not something quickly turned out as a rubber-stamped document of little value. The entire plan for the child goes in the IEP, and you are guaranteed to see the IEP evaluated by others if the parents attack the child's educational activities. As much work as it is to produce a good IEP, it is still far less work than the hundreds of hours needed to defend that document in court. It is worth doing the IEP correctly the first time.

One of the best sources for detailed information on drafting an IEP is found in the Code of Federal Regulations as "Appendix A to Part 300," which describes the requirements and answers to frequently asked questions encountered in IEPs, including how to write an IEP. The Appendix is a little hard to find, and is attached to the end of Title 34, Regulation 300.756 (34 CFR 300.756).] It is also reprinted in full in this book as Chapter **7**.

Because this Appendix is so hard to find, the author suggests a Google search for "interpretation of IEP and other selected requirements under Part B" and select one of the websites to the federal register.

Chapter Twelve

Court Case of When There is a Change in Circumstances Requiring an IEP

Concerned Parents v. New York City Bd. Of Ed.
629 F.2d 751 (1980)

Facts of Case

This case focuses on when an IEP is needed. For budget reasons a New York School District closed a school (P.S. 79) and transferred all the students to other schools within the same district. Approximately 60% of the school was composed of handicapped students, who were transferred without an IEP notice or a chance to object. Further, although the classes they were sent to were rated on paper and approximately equal, many did not match the superior, innovative programs of the old P.S. 79 school. The parents sued.

There were many issues decided by the court, and only selected portions of Circuit Judge Feinberg's judicial decision are reported below.

Note that all citations are left out and notations indicating missing text have been omitted to make the reading easier.

The Purpose of IDEA Notice. Why is notice to the parents of such importance under the IDEA?

"The primary purpose of the Act is to encourage states, through the use of fiscal incentives, to provide a "free appropriate public education" for all handicapped children. In furtherance of this goal, the Act also embodies a range of procedures designed to ensure that fundamental decisions concerning the education of handicapped children are made correctly and with appropriate input from the parents or guardians of such children.

[As an example,] pursuant to 20 U.S.C. §1415(b) (1)(C), whenever, an educational agency covered by the Act (i) proposes to initiate or change or (ii) refuses to initiate or change the identification, evaluation, or educational and placement of the child or the provision of a free appropriate education to the child, it must provide the parents or guardian of the child with prior written notice. Other subsections of §1415(b) require the agency to provide parents or guardians in such cases with an opportunity for "an impartial due process hearing."

[Providing notice then becomes one of the major protections and cornerstones of IDEA. It is only through this notice that parents can protect themselves and their educationally disabled children and ensure that they receive a "free" and "appropriate" education.]"

Intra-District Transfer To Similar Program OK. The IDEA is very clear that any change in program of a handicapped student requires an IEP, which if the parents object, provides the parents with a host of remedies

anc protections. The parents felt that since the school their children were sent to did not equal the unusually creative and effective approach of the older P.S. 79, an IEP meeting was required. This would necessitate a hearing and a change for the parents to object by using the full force of the objection provisions contained in the Individuals With Disabilities Education Act. The court had to decide if such notice and rights needed to be granted to the parents.

"On the record before us, it is clear that the transfer of students from P.S. 79 was poorly planned, and that the move was disconcerting to many of the handicapped children that had attended the school. Moreover, as the district court found, the schools to which the students were transferred do not, in all respects duplicate the 'extremely innovative educational program' formerly provided to handicapped children at P.S 79.

However, the issue before us is not whether the Board acted wisely or carried out its decision properly. Instead, the narrow question is whether the transfer cf handicapped children in special classes at one school to substantially similar classes at other schools within the same school district constitutes a change in 'placement' sufficient to trigger the Act's prior notice and hearing requirements.

The statute fails to define 'change…in educational placement.' We believe the term refers only to the general type of educational program in which the child is placed. Several factors support this conclusion. First, in §1415(b)(1)(C) the term 'educational placement' is used in the context of changes in the 'identification, evaluation, or educational placement' of the handicapped child.

This language suggests that the full notice and hearing requirements of §1415(b) were limited to certain fundamental decisions regarding the existence and classification of a handicap, and the most appropriate type of educational program for assisting a child with such a handicap.

The legislative history of the Act supports this interpretation, for it indicates that a primary concern of Congress in enacting these procedural protections of §1415(b) was to prevent the erroneous identification or, classification of children as handicapped and the impairment of their subsequent education by ensuring that parents would be afforded prior notice and an opportunity to participate in such fundamental determinations. Thus the reference to 'educational placement' in §1415(b)(1)(C) would appear to, refer to the general educational program in which a child who is correctly identified, as handicapped is enrolled, rather than mere variations in the program itself.

Thus, the regulations use the term 'placement' to refer only to the general educational programs provided for handicapped children, and the reference to a "change" in 'educational placement' in §1415(b)(1) (C) would therefore apparently encompass only decisions to transfer a child from one type of program to another. For example, a decision to transfer a handicapped child from a special class in a regular school to a special school would involve the sort of fundamental alteration in the child's education requiring prior parental notification under §1415(b).

Thus, we conclude that the term 'educational placement' refers on the general educational program in which the handicapped child is placed and not to all the various adjustments in that program. The educational agency, in the traditional exercise of its discretion, [make such adjustments in that program as it] may determine to be necessary. Accordingly, we conclude that the Board was not required under the Act to give the parents of handicapped children at P.S. 79 prior notice and a full due process hearing before the transfer."

Examples of Acts Requiring Notice under

IDEA. This case only gave one example of the type of educational placement that required an IEP and notice to the parents. However, other cases from across the United States have also offered guidelines. A few of the cases that have held notice was or was not required are below. This part below is from the author and not the court.

Not be transferred from special class in a regular school to a special School.

A decision to transfer a handicapped child from a special class in a regular school to a special school would involve the sort of fundamental alteration in the child's education requiring prior parental notification.[1]

Not be expelled from school for acts related to disability.

The rule is that handicapped students cannot be expelled or permanently excluded from school for any misconduct that is a result of their handicap. The courts have specifically ruled that California Education Code providing for suspension of students in general is inapplicable as to such disabled students.[2]

Note, however, the child may be expelled for acts unrelated to their impediment.[3]

Not be suspended from school for more than 10 days related to disability.

Suspension differs from expulsion, and a child may be suspended for up to 10 days for acts related to that child's disability. Upon return to school, the student must be returned to the educational environment existing before his suspension (the "stay put"

---

1. *Concerned Parents v. New York City Bd. Of Ed.* 629 F.2d 751 (1980), by dicta.
2. *Doe By Gonzales v. Maher* 793 F.2d 1470, 1484 (9th Cir. 1986).
3. *California Education Code §48915.5*

provisions of the IDEA), unless and until a new IEP is done.

The regulation permitting this 10-day suspension, holds that under certain circumstances the 10 days can be cumulative, and need not be consecutive. 34 CRF 300.519, the federal regulation controlling this subject, holds that a change of placement occurs if the "child is subjected to a series of removals that constitute a pattern because they cumulate to more than 10 school days in a school year, and because of factors such as the length of each removal, the total amount of time the child is removed, and the proximity of the removals to one another."

Note, however, that a child may be suspended for 10 days or less for acts related to their disability, or may be suspended for longer periods for acts totally unrelated to their impediment.

Not change classification of disability. Changing a child's disability from a learning disability to an emotional handicap is a change in educational placement requiring prior notice under IDEA.[1]

Not graduate student if graduation causes loss of special education services. The decision to graduate a handicapped child cannot be done except with notice to the parents under IDEA if that graduation will cause the student's ability to participate in special education services.[1] There is some uncertainty if a mere graduation that will not result in loss of special education services requires coverage under IDEA.

Examples of Acts Not Requiring Notice under IDEA. Notice is required for placement in a handicapped class or for changes to the general educational program in which that hand-

---

1. *Davis v. Maine Endwell Cent. School Dist.* (1982, ND NY) 542 F.Supp. 1257.

icapped child is enrolled. However, IDEA notice is not required for mere variations in the program, itself. A few of the cases that have held an act was not under IDEA and therefore did not need advance notice are stated below.

Transfer to similar class within the district

. The transfer of handicapped students from one special class to another, substantially similar special class within the same district was not a change in educational placement for which an IEP was required.[1]

Suspension for acts related to disabilities

. Even though students may not be expelled for acts related to their disabilities, they may be suspended a provided by the California Education Code §43910 (which allows for two-day suspensions by their teacher) and by §48911 (which allows for a five-day suspension by their principal).[2]

Remember that the Act actually allows up to a 10-day suspension as is explained under the third example under *Acts Requiring Notice* above.

Expulsion for acts not arising from disability

. The rule is that handicapped students can be expelled for misconduct that is a unrelated and not result of their handicap. However to do so, is a "change in placement" which requires due process under IDEA, and during the time until the matter is settled, the student must remain where he is ("stay-put provisions").[3]

Lesson from this Case

1. *Concernea Parents v. New York City Bd. Of Ed.* 629 F.2d 751 (1980), Weil v. Bd. of Elementary & Secondary Educ., C.A.5(La.), 931 F.2d 1069
2. *Doe By Gonzales v. Maher*, 793 F.2d 1470, 1481 (9th Cir. 1986).
3. *Doe By Gonzales v. Maher*, 793 F.2d 1470, 1481 (9th Cir. 1986).

It is very difficult to form hard and fast rules when an action is totally exempt from the provisions of IDEA because the facts of each case can vary so significantly. The purpose of IDEA is to provide an appropriate education for disabled students and to allow the parents to monitor that education by providing adequate notice and rights to independent evaluations of the child. Because of the consequences of failing to follow the act, it is the author's suggestion that if in doubt, assume IDEA applies.

Conducting Further Research

The article *Changes in Educational Placement* (54 ALR Fed 570) is an excellent resource to begin research on this issues discussed above. Go to any law library near you and ask the librarian to find and pull the above book for you. When you have the volume, turn to page 570 for the beginning of the discussion.

COURT CASE OF CHILD QUALIFYING UNDER IDEA EVEN THOUGH SCHOOL DID NOT DIAGNOSE A DISABILITY

Hacienda La Puente Sch. Dist. of L.A. v. Honig 976 F.2d 487 (9th Cir. 1992)

Facts of Case

A student (identified only by the initials "B.C.") began seventh grade in 1988 at the Hacienda La Puente Unified School District in Los Angeles County. B.C. was a marginal student, who was sometimes oppositionally defiant and in trouble. A year later his new adopted mother complained to the vice-principal about her sons academic progress and inappropriate behavior. The school held an informal student study team evaluation, which recommended a "homework contract" and some counseling. Later that year the mother specifically requested an evaluation for special education services. The school tested B.C. and found he did not qualify for special education.

The mother then had B.C. tested by her experts who found B.C. to be disabled. The school reevaluated B.C. and again found he was not disabled or qualified for special education. Later that year B.C. was suspended for fighting and the school began proceedings to expel him. At that point B.C.'s parents hired an attorney who brought this action claiming B.C. was disabled, qualified for special education, and could not be expelled because his behavior was the result of his disability.

One of the positions taken by the school was that B.C. was not disabled and therefore did not fall within IDEA and its provisions.

The Court Decision

Can Be IDEA Qualified Even if the School Determines the Student is Not Disabled. If the school does a good faith evaluation of a student, in this case B.C., and finds he is not disabled, can the courts later find the child was disabled?

> "[The school district claims that] because the IDEA most often refers to 'children with disabilities' and, in its former statutory incarnation, to 'handicapped children,' it is necessary for a school district or similar agency to identify a child as 'disabled' or 'handicapped' before the procedural safeguards mandated by [IDEA] can be invoked.
>
> We reject this argument. The IDEA and accompanying federal regulations, as well as California law, make plain that, even though not previously identified as disabled, the student's alleged disability may be raised in an IDEA administrative due process hearing.
>
> IDEA requires that states participating in IDEA entertain complaints respecting any matter relating to the identification of the child. [The code of fed-

eral regulations even permits a] parent to initiate a hearing when school district refuses either to initiate or change the identification of a student as disabled). The language of these statutes necessarily encompasses a complaint based on a school district's refusal to identify a child as disabled. [In other words, parents or guardians can sue the school district for not recognizing their child as qualified under IDEA.]

A contrary result would frustrate the core purpose of the IDEA, which is to prevent schools from indiscriminately excluding disabled students from educational opportunities. In enacting the IDEA, Congress specifically recognized that undetected disabilities prevent many children from "having a successful educational experience."

If we [the court] found issues concerning the detection of disabilities to be outside the scope of IDEA "due process hearings," school districts could easily circumvent the statute's requirements by refusing to identify students as disabled."

Still Be Expelled. Can a student, in this case B.C., be expelled if the expulsion request was made before he was considered disabled?

"In support of its argument, the school district points to various provisions of California Education Code. This statute prescribes procedures by which disabled students might be expelled from California public schools. The provisions on which the school district relies refer to 'pupils with previously identified exceptional needs.' The School District argues that because B.C. had not previously been identified as having exceptional needs or otherwise being disabled, he had no right to an administrative due process hearing.

As the School District interprets the statute, it is inconsistent with the federal statutory and regulatory law by which California has chosen to abide. [Indeed,

California must follow federal law in this regard. Further, the California Education Code provides that no student with special needs can be expelled until there has been a preexplusion assessment, then an IEP team evaluation that the misconduct in question was not a result of the child's handicap, and finally all appropriate due process hearings have been completed.]

The Supreme Court in affirming our decision emphasized that in passing IDEA, 'Congress very much meant to strip schools of their unilateral authority they had traditionally employed to exclude disabled students, particularly emotionally disturbed students, from school.'

The Supreme Court leaves the unmistakable impression that all disabled students, whether or not possessing "previously identified exceptional needs, are entitled to the protections afforded under the IDEA. [Thus, B.C. can not be expelled if he is disabled, as was found, if his behavior was the result of his diagnosed disability. Review the notes from the last case in this booklet on the rights to suspend and expel a disabled student.]"

Lesson from this Case

Be very careful if a parent presents you with evidence that a child is disabled, even if you do not find him so. If you are wrong, as in this case, the parents are entitled to attorney's fees as well as the cost of an appropriate education until the school so provides.

Additionally, a student may be disabled under the much broader section 504 of the Rehabilitation Act (commonly referred to as a "Section 504" disability). Section 504 is discussed in chapter **14** of this book.

PART IV

SECTION 504 PLANS AND LAW

CHAPTER FOURTEEN

SUMMARY OF SECTION 504 LAW

Section 504" Concerns

Even though section 504 of the federal Rehabilitation Act[1] is not part of IDEA, it is imperative to understand §504 to know when IDEA might not apply but section 504 would.[2] As this chapter will discuss, Section 504's definition of disability is far broader and more encompassing than IDEA, so students might find coverage under its provisions.[3] While a section 504 student would have far fewer rights and in-

---

1. Since January 1, 2009 the Americans with Disabilities Act of 1990 ("ADA") amended Section 504 of the Rehabilitation Act of 1973 ("Section 504"). The ADA broadened the types of disabilities qualifying for Section 504, but otherwise made no major changes. In fact, the federal regulations concerning educational institutions remains unchanged. The regulations are at 34 C.F.R. Part 104.

2. Section 504 provides: "No otherwise qualified individual with a disability in the United States ... shall, solely by reason of her or his disability, be excluded from the participation in, be denied the benefits of, or be subjected to discrimination under any program or activity receiving Federal financial assistance ...." The code is found at 29 U.S.C. § 794 (Section 504).

3. As do regulations concerning other code sections, Section 504 requires school districts to provide a "free appropriate public education" often abbreviated as FAPE. In summary, each qualified disabled student must be given the same aids, support and services as required to receive FAPE as would be received by a nondisabled student. The school district can in no way discriminate against a qualified disabled student.

terventions than IDEA, the student would still have certain procedural safeguards.

If you are presented with a medical report that the child is disabled, you should immediately think the student could be covered under Section 504. If you suspect the child is disabled under Section 504 and there is no diagnosis supporting that position, you may wish to meet with the parents to ask if there are medical reports that could be released with their permission. If the parent say the child has not been so diagnosed, be sure to document that discussion so there is a paper trail.

In one case involving IDEA the United States Supreme Court ruled that a school district not finding a child qualified for special services under IDEA could be held liable if the student should have been so qualified. Here the child was later found to have had Attention Deficit Hyperactivity Disease ("ADHD") and the school district was asked to reimburse the parents the costs of the child's tuition at a private school. The school district could be held liable if the district failed to provide a FAPE even though the child was never diagnosed by the school district as being IDEA qualified.[1] Under these rationale, the logic and law of the case should also apply to Section 504 children.[1]

Definition of Disability

Section 504 defines a handicap, even if that handicap does not affect the child's learning and educational process. A child is handicapped if he or she "(i) has a physical or mental impairment which substantially limits one or more of such person's major life activities, (ii) has a record of such an impairment, or (iii) is regarded as having such impairment."

Basically, impairment is a disability, illness, or condition that "substantially" reduces the student's ability to receive an appropriate education. It is not enough that a student have a physical or mental impairment; that impairment must be

---

1.   Forest Grove School District v. T. A., 557 U.S. ___, 129 S.Ct. 2484 (2009)

of such severity that it results in a substantial limitation of at least one of that child's major life activities. The major life activity may be a heart condition, hearing impairment, allergy, poor eyesight, or any other physical or mental condition that substantially limits the student's ability to receive an appropriate education.

Every child who qualifies for IDEA is also disabled under Section 504. However, not every child who is Section 504 disabled is disabled under IDEA. Briefly, under IDEA the disability must affect a student's right to free, appropriate, public education that is provided by special education and related services. However, under Section 504, the disability generally does not adversely affect a student's education performance.

Typical section 504 disabilities that are not covered under IDEA include attention conditions (like ADD or ADHA) and physical conditions (like asthma or a severely deformed limb).

Purpose And Procedure

The main purpose of Section 504 of the Rehabilitation Act is to include and integrate disabled people into mainstream society. Section 504 provides that no one with a disability

> "shall, solely by reason of her or his disability, be excluded from the participation in, be denied the benefits of, or be subject to discrimination under any program or activity receiving Federal financial assistance"

which includes schools. Section 504 prevents such schools from discriminating against disabled students and requires them to provide "access" to a free, appropriate education that is "as adequate" as that given to nonhandicapped people.

In other words, the schools must offer "reasonable accommodations" to insure handicapped student's educational opportunities are the same as those of regular students. To accomplish this, the schools must generally develop a section 504 plan for the disabled student.

§504 Goal Less Powerful Than IDEA

Section 504 is an anti-discrimination statute. When applied to education, §504 requires schools to provide school ramps for wheelchair students, and to make other reasonable accommodations for handicapped students to equalize their educational opportunities. However, it is not designed to increase a student's abilities over that of other students. There is no "individualized educational program," enhancing a child's educational development. **The section 504 plan only equalizes the child's opportunity for an education free of discrimination.** It's educational accommodations are general when compared to the specifics of IDEA.

Court Case Involving Section 504

J.D was an academically gifted high school student (an IQ test placed him in the top two percent of his age group). He also had certain emotional and behavioral problems, steaming from "boredom, alienation, apathy and hopelessness because of an absence of intellectual peers" at his high school. J.D.'s parents requested an evaluation for special education.[1]

The school team found J.D. was not qualified for special education under IDEA because he did not need remedial education as his superior grades demonstrated. However, the team did find that J.D. was "disabled" under section 504 of the Rehabilitation Act. The section 504 plan included individual counseling and the ability to sit in classes for older students.

His parents did not agree with the section 504 plan, and removed J.D. from public school. They sent him to an exclusive, out-of-state boarding school for academically gifted

---

1. *J.D. Ex. Rel. J. D. v. Pawlet School Dist.* 224 F.3d 60 (2nd Cir. 2000).

students. The parents then sent the school a bill asking them to pay the cost of J.D.'s education.

The court sided with school system, finding the 504 plan resulted in educational opportunity that was equal to that of a non-disabled student.

Like IDEA, section 504 only requires an "appropriate" education, not the best education available. The parents had to pay for J.D.'s private schooling.

Comparison to IDEA

	§504 of the Rehabilitation Act	**IDEA**
Covers	Regulates many organizations (including schools) that receive federal funds.	Affects schools that educate children with certain specified disabilities.
Purpose	This is a broad civil rights type act that protects people with disabilities.	Provides a free and appropriate education to disabled children.
Funding	No additional funding of this Act.	Direct federal funding to states for use in ensuring that its disabled students receive educational assistance.
Who Covered	Person who has a physical or mental impairment that limits one or more major life activities, or has a record of such disability, or is regarded as having an impairment.	A school aged student who falls into one or more of the 14 disability categories under IDEA.

	§504 of the Rehabilitation Act	IDEA
Student Needs Written Plan	Statute just requires adequate documentation of evaluation. Normally, this involves so sort of Section 504 written plan.	Formal written Individualized Education Program (IEP) according to statute, and, if qualified behavioral problems, a Behavioral Intervention Plan (BIP).
Definition of Disability	The physical or mental impairment that limits major life activity in walking, seeing, hearing, breathing, learning, speaking, or working.	The student has intellectual disabilities, hearing impairment, speech or language impairment, visual impairment, serious emotional disturbances, orthopedic impairment, autism, traumatic brain injury, other health impairment, deafness, deaf-blind, multiple disabilities, specific learning disabilities, intellectual disability, or developmental delay.

	§504 of the Reha-bilitation Act	**IDEA**
Services Required	Requires reasonable accommodation, which for students can also mean aids and other support so child benefit from general education.	Must provide all services specified in the IEP and/or BIP, such as speech and language specialist, special instruction, aide, transportation, even physical or occupational thera-pists.
References	29 USC 794 34 CFR Part 104	20 USC 1400 et seq. 34 CFR Parts 300 & 303

PART V

BEHAVIORAL INTERVENTION

CHAPTER FIFTEEN

COURT CASE OF INADEQUATE BEHAVIOR MODIFICATION PLAN

Chris D. v. Montgomery County Bd. of Educ. 753 F.Supp. 922 (M.D. Ala. 1990)

Importance of Behavioral Plans

Behavioral Assessment Plans are an integral and necessary part of an IEP for a disabled child with a behavioral problem that affects his or her education. Don't get caught without one.

In September, 2002, American Bar Association's presented a nation-wide broadcast for attorneys who representation of students with disabilities. The panelists of leading experts all agreed that statistically clients are most often driven to seek legal help when the school districts begin disciplinary actions against their child.

During the initial attorney-client meeting, one of the key points attorneys representing clients should look for in such situations is the Behavioral Intervention Plan.

Facts of Case

Corry was a student with a severe emotional problem which affected his already poor academic performance. He repeated forth grade, but was finally placed in an educably mentally retarded class. In fifth grade the parents had Corry professionally evaluated and their professional found Corry was not mentally retarded, and that he needed a self-contained classroom for emotionally conflicted children. Corry's disruptive behavior to teachers and pupils resulted in considerable punishment, but little improvement in Corry's performance or behavior. Corry had a dismal fifth grade year.

Sixth grade was a repeat of the earlier year, and Corry was amply punished for his behavior. Finally, the parents filed for a due process hearing, which was ultimately appealed to this court. The court found for Corry's parents, holding the IEP failed to include a meaningful behavioral modification plan objectives and failed to instruct the parents in how to help Corry.

Court Decision

Rewards And Punishments Inadequate. The IEP contained a few, broad goals about Corry's behavior, but little else. Corry's teachers adopted a plan of rewarding Corry's good behavior and punishing his bad behavior. Unfortunately, his negative behavior predominated, and he was often and significantly disciplined. Except for the rewards and punishment, there was little else done to work with Corry's behavior problems. The Court considered if this approach was adequate, especially in light of the almost non-existent behavior modification plan which should have been part of the IEP.

> There is ample evidence that Corry's emotional disability is primarily responsible for his academic problems. His inability to stay on task, to obey directions, or to avoid disrupting a class has obviously contributed significantly to Corry's learning difficulties.

The system of behavioral control which Corry's teachers have implemented since that time has been woefully inadequate. The evidence reflects that school system officials have sought to keep Corry quiet and hidden away from other students, rather than attempting to teach him to control his own behavior, an essential approach to educating emotionally conflicted children.

The few behavioral "goals" contained in Corry's most recent IEP actually describe only general classroom rules and the punishments and rewards for breaking or following these rules, rather than any individualized strategies for changing Corry's behavior.

In his testimony, Batsche [a nationally recognized psychologist hired by Corry's parents] stated categorically that such a generalized, "reinforcement" approach for coping with emotionally conflicted children was uniformly rejected by educators approximately ten years ago. According to Batsche, the only method for addressing the behavioral problems of such children that is currently accepted and whose results are proven is one which seeks to teach them the skills necessary for controlling their own conduct. As Batsche explained, attempting to teach Corry appropriate behavior by means of reinforcement is comparable to trying to teach a child to swim by throwing him in the water and offering to reward him for not drowning.

Furthermore, the absence of specific behavioral objectives in Corry's present or past IEP's makes it virtually impossible for special education personnel to determine why or how Corry misbehaves or to evaluate whether particular educational strategies are actually having an impact on particular forms of misbehavior.

Are Notes Home To Parents Adequate. Corry's teacher sent frequent notes to the parents indicating Corry's classroom work and behavior, which the parents had to sign.

Otherwise, there was little parental involvement in Corry's school behavior. The court found such lack of training totally inadequate.

> Finally, school system officials have ignored another crucial component of a proper behavioral control program by failing to counsel and instruct Corry's parents in how to complement at home the training Corry receives at school. It is well established that a "free appropriate public education" under the Act includes not only specially designed educational instruction, but also such related services "as are necessary to permit the child 'to benefit' from the instruction."
>
> The EHA defines "related services" broadly, and the federal regulations implementing the Act specifically include, among these services, "parent counseling and training," which is defined as "assisting parents in understanding the special needs of their child and providing parents with information about child development."

Shouldn't Parents Have A Responsibility.

Educating the child and providing an academically appropriate environment lies predominately with the schools. This includes meeting the child's emotional and behavioral problems that affect a disabled child's education. The school cannot just abrogate this obligation to the parents and ignore their own accountability or responsibility.

> The school board has suggested that mental health and other counseling services are available to Corry's family from agencies in the community. However, the [IDEA] Act requires that school officials, themselves arrange to provide necessary "related services" to a handicapped child and that the IEP describe the services to be offered.

Lessons From this Case
and Cases Like It

An Appropriate Behavioral Intervention Plan. What is a behavioral intervention plan and what must it include? California Code of Regulations, Title 5, Section 3001(f) contains a good, clear definition and description of its components. [The subparagraph headings are the author's, and not part of the regulations.]

> Behavioral intervention plan is a written document which is developed when the individual exhibits a serious behavior problem that significantly interferes with the implementation of the goals and objectives of the individual's IEP. The "behavioral intervention plan" shall become part of the IEP. The plan shall describe the frequency of the consultation to be provided by the behavioral intervention case manager to the staff members and parents who are responsible for implementing the plan.
>
> A copy of the plan shall be provided to the person or agency responsible for implementation in noneducational settings. The plan shall include the following:

> (1) **Functional Analysis Summary**. A summary of relevant and determinative information gathered from a functional analysis assessment;

> (2) **Measurable Descriptions**. An objective and measurable description of the targeted maladaptive behavior(s) and replacement positive behavior(s);

> (3) **Goals and Objectives**. The individual's goals and objectives specific to the behavioral intervention plan;

(4) **Descriptions of Intervention**. A detailed description of the behavioral interventions to be used and the circumstances for their use;

(5) **Time Lines**. Specific schedules for recording the frequency of the use of the interventions and the frequency of the targeted and replacement behaviors; including specific criteria for discontinuing the use of the intervention for lack of effectiveness or replacing it with an identified and specified alternative;

(6) **Phase Out Plans**. Criteria by which the procedure will be faded or phased-out, or less intense/frequent restrictive behavioral intervention schedules or techniques will be used;

(7) **Off-Site Interventions**. Those behavioral interventions which will be used in the home, residential facility, work site or other noneducational settings; and

(8) **Review Dates**. Specific dates for periodic review by the IEP team of the efficacy of the program.

When Behavioral Intervention Plan Must Be Done.

When is a behavioral intervention plan required to be prepared? What seems like a surprisingly easy question is actually more difficult than it might appear at first glance.

The IDEA is relatively silent, except for a brief paragraph in the codes concerning discipline of a disabled student. 20 UCS 1415(k)(1)(B).

The California regulations state that a "functional analysis assessment shall occur after the individualized education program team finds that instructional/behavioral approaches specified in the student's IEP have been ineffective. Nothing in this section shall preclude a parent or legal guardian from requesting a functional analysis assessment [pursuant to law]." California Code of regulations, Title 5, Section 3052(b).

Under California regulations, once a functional analysis assessment has been completed, then an "IEP team meeting shall be held to review results and, if necessary, to develop a behavioral intervention plan" California Code of regulations, Title 5, Section 3052(c).

These California regulations define a behavioral intervention plan as "a written document which is developed when the individual exhibits a serious behavior problem that significantly interferes with the implementation of the goals and objectives of the individual's IEP." California Code of regulations, Title 5, Section 3001(f).

It is the author's belief that as soon as it becomes apparent that a disabled child might have a serious behavior problem that affects his education, the school should begin a functional analysis assessment to determine if, in fact, the student does indeed have such a behavior problem. If so, then strategies, goals and objectives of a written behavioral intervention plan should be included in the IEP.

Finally, disciplinary placements in alternative education settings require special consideration. Whenever the school plans to take a action against a disabled student "to an appropriate interim alternative educational settings, another setting, or suspension, for not more than 10 school days [or up to 45 days if weapons or drugs are involved] to the extent that such alternatives would be applied to children without disabilities" the school needs to consider a functional behavioral assessment as stated below. 20 USC 1415(k).

No Prior Behavioral Assessment Plan.
"Either before or not later than 10 days after taking a disciplinary action ... if the local educational agency did not conduct a functional behavioral assessment and implement a behavioral intervention plan for such child before the behavior that result in the [suspension/discipline], the agency shall convene an IEP meeting to develop an assessment plan to address that behavior."

Existing Behavioral Assessment Plan.
"Either before or not later than 10 days after taking a disciplinary action ... the IEP Team shall review the plan and modify it, as necessary, to address the behavior."

Requirement When Behavior Extreme

In a separate lawsuit by Chris D.'s parents, they claim the school district failed to provide Chris a free appropriate public education" as required under the Education of the Handicapped Act (EHA). Chris' behavior disrupted his classes, resulted in frequent referral to the principal's office, physical altercations occasionally required police intervention, frequent use of profanity in class upset the classroom, and repeated beating on the walls of the principal's office when called there for disciplining. The mother finally sued claiming Chris needed the special attention of a full time residential program for which she wanted the school district to pay. The court analyzed the request and the school district's alternative of special day classes or home tutoring. *Chris d. V. Montgomery County Bd. of Educ.* 743 F.Supp. 1524 (1990). In that case the court held:

The EHA provides federal funds to assist state and local governments in educating handicapped children. As a condition for funding, states are required to provide a "free appropriate public education" for all disabled children within their jurisdictions. [Procedurally] "the Act establishes a comprehensive system of procedural safeguards designed to ensure parental participation in decisions concerning the education of their disabled children and to provide administrative and judicial review of any decisions with which those parents disagree." [Substantively] a disabled student has a right to "personalized instruction with sufficient support services to permit the child to benefit educationally from the instruction," [as well as] a right to be "mainstreamed" — that is, placed in the "least restrictive environment" possible.

Under this requirement, a handicapped child may be removed from the regular classroom setting "only when the nature or severity of the handicap is such that education in regular classes with the use of supplementary aids and services cannot be achieved satisfactorily.

The expert testimony is undisputed that behavior modification is an essential element of any placement program for Chris. The chief impediment to Chris's ability to function academically in the school system is his inability to control his behavior. Unless and until his behavior is controlled, he will not be able to function at all in the school system, let alone in a regular classroom setting. This fact is made evident by his suspensions from Bear Elementary because of severe disruptive behavior. The evidence is also clear that Chris's behavior problems cannot be redressed in an isolated environment. Any behavior modification program for Chris must include interaction with his peers.

It is apparent that the thrust of the school board's proposals is to hide Chris away so that he cannot disrupt the on-going education of other students. The true intended beneficiary of the proposals is the school system and not Chris. The school board overlooks, however, that, as with most hidden human problems, Chris's problems will not go away — they will only grow worse.

The school board correctly observes that the EHA requires that a school district provide only "educational benefit." The school board argues that Chris will receive some educational benefit under either of their two proposals of homebound instruction or individual instruction in an administrative building. The court cannot agree. Under the test the school board is implicitly proffering, a benefit is conferred anytime a student is not left to vegetate.

Having carefully considered the school system's proposed placements and all the evidence presented by both parties, the court concludes that Chris should be enrolled immediately in a full-time residential school [at the District's cost] in order to receive the individual instruction and special services necessary for him to receive any benefit educationally.

Chapter Sixteen

Behavioral Interventions in Callifornia

Common Encounter in Law with Disciplinary Issues

California's regulations probably parallel those in other states, although a careful check is required to ascertain any deviations.

This chapter places special emphasis on behavior modification plans and their limitations because such plans can be so closely tied in with IEPs. Indeed, 5 CCR §3502(a)(3) mandates that behavior assessment plans are included in the IEP.

In is interesting to note that during a September, 2002, American Bar Association's nation-wide broadcast on attorney's representation of students with disabilities, several key panelists stated that the majority clients are seeking legal representation for disciplinary action taken by the schools.

One of the key points attorneys look for in such situations is the *Behavioral Intervention Plan*. Residents of California looking for behavioral interventions need to realize the requirements are found in the *California Code of Regulations* and not in the *Education Code*.

Not every regulation is included below. The author chose only selected regulations that seemed most relevant for the reader. Many of the regulations below have subtitles that have been added by the author. Titles and subtitles make the regulations easier to read, but should be ignored in evaluating a regulation's legal import.

Anyone wanting to reading a full list of all regulations should go to their local law librarian and ask the librarian for Title 5 of the *California Code of Regulations.*

The text below also includes regulations relating to individuals with exceptional needs since behavioral intervention does not occur in a vacuum. Anyone seeking to discipline a student needs to know if that pupil qualifies for and is considered as a student with exceptional needs.

CALIFORNIA CODE OF REGULATIONS

In California the regulations implementing and defining in detail the requirements of federal law and of California state law, specifically the California Education Code, are found in Title 5 of the California Code of Regulations. The California Code of Regulations is often abbreviated as CCR. Thus, a citation of 5 CCR §3001 means the text is located in Title 5 of the California Code of Regulations in Section 3001.

5 CCR 3001 — DEFINITIONS

(d) **Definition of Behavioral Emergency**. "Behavioral emergency" is the demonstration of a serious behavior problem: (1) which has not previously been observed and for which a behavioral intervention plan has not been developed; or (2) for which a previously designed behavioral intervention is not effective. Approved behavioral emergency procedures must be outlined in the special education local planning area (SELPA) local plan.

(e) **Definition of Behavioral Intervention**. "Behavioral intervention" means the systematic implementation of procedures that result in lasting positive changes in the individual's behavior. "Behavioral intervention" means the design, implementation, and evaluation of individual or group instructional and environmental modifications, including programs of behavioral instruction, to produce significant improvements in human behavior through skill acquisition and the reduction of problematic behavior. "Behavioral interventions" are designed to provide the individual with greater access to a variety of community settings, social contacts and public events; and ensure the individual's right to placement in the least restrictive educational environment as outlined in the individual's IEP. "Behavioral interventions" do not include procedures, which cause pain or trauma. "Behavioral interventions" respect the individual's human dignity and personal privacy. Such interventions shall assure the individual's physical freedom, social interaction, and individual choice.

(f) **Definition of Behavioral Intervention Case Manager.** "Behavioral intervention case manager" means a designated certificated school/district/county/nonpublic school or agency staff member(s) or other qualified personnel pursuant to subdivision (ac) contracted by the school district or county office or nonpublic school or agency who has been trained in behavior analysis with an emphasis on positive behavioral interventions. The "behavioral intervention case manager" is not intended to be a new staffing requirement and does not create any new credentialing or degree requirements. The duties of the "behavioral intervention case manager" may be performed by any existing staff member trained in behavioral analysis with an emphasis on positive behavioral interventions, including, but not limited to, a teacher, resource specialist, school psychologist, or program specialist.

(g) **Definition of Behavioral Intervention Plan**. "Behavioral intervention plan" is a written document which is developed when the individual exhibits a serious behavior problem that significantly interferes with the implementation of the goals and objectives of the individual's

IEP. The "behavioral intervention plan" shall become part of the IEP. The plan shall describe the frequency of the consultation to be provided by the behavioral intervention case manager to the staff members and parents who are responsible for implementing the plan. A copy of the plan shall be provided to the person or agency responsible for implementation in noneducational settings. The plan shall include the following:

(1) **Functional Analysis Assessment**. a summary of relevant and determinative information gathered from a functional analysis assessment;

(2) **Measurable Descriptions.** an objective and measurable description of the targeted maladaptive behavior(s) and replacement positive behavior(s);

(3) **Goals and Objectives.** the individual's goals and objectives specific to the behavioral intervention plan;

(4) **Descriptions of Intervention**. a detailed description of the behavioral interventions to be used and the circumstances for their use;

(5) **Time Lines**. specific schedules for recording the frequency of the use of the interventions and the frequency of the targeted and replacement behaviors; including specific criteria for discontinuing the use of the intervention for lack of effectiveness or replacing it with an identified and specified alternative;

(6) **Phase Out Plans**. criteria by which the procedure will be faded or phased-out, or less intense/ frequent restrictive behavioral intervention schedules or techniques will be used;

(7) **Off-Site Interventions**. those behavioral inter-

ventions which will be used in the home, residential facility, work site or other noneducational settings; and

(8) **Review Dates**. specific dates for periodic review by the IEP team of the efficacy of the program.

(aa) **Definition of Related Services**. "Related services" means transportation, and such developmental, corrective, and other supportive services (including speech pathology and audiology, psychological services, physical and occupational therapy, recreation, including therapeutic recreation, social work services, counseling services, including rehabilitation counseling, and medical services. except that such medical services shall be for diagnostic and evaluation purposes only) as required to assist an individual with exceptional needs to benefit from special education, and includes the early identification and assessment of disabling conditions in children. Related services include, but are not limited to, designated instruction and services. The list of related services is not exhaustive and may include other developmental, corrective, or supportive services if they are required to assist a child with a disability to benefit from special education. Each related service defined under this part may include appropriate administrative and supervisory activities that are necessary for program planning, management, and evaluation.

(ab) **Definition of Serious Behavior Problems**. "Serious behavior problems" means the individual's behaviors which are self-injurious, assaultive, or cause serious property damage and other severe behavior problems that are pervasive and maladaptive for which instructional/behavioral approaches specified in the student's IEP are found to be ineffective.

(ac) **Definition of Special Education**. "Special education" means specially designed instruction, at no cost to the parents, to meet the unique needs of individuals with exceptional needs whose educational needs cannot be met with modification of the regular instruction program, and related services, at no cost to the parent, that may be needed to assist these individuals to benefit from specially designed instruction.

5 CCR 3030 – Eligibility Criteria. Individuals with Exceptional Needs

Definition of Individual with Exceptional Needs. A pupil shall qualify as an individual with exceptional needs, pursuant to Section 56026 of the Education Code, if the results of the assessment as required by Section 56320 demonstrate that the degree of the pupil's impairment as described in Section 3030 (a through j) requires special education in one or more of the program options authorized by Section 56361 of the Education Code. The decision as to the whether or not the assessment results demonstrate that the degree of the pupil's impairment requires special education shall be made by the individualized education program team, including personnel in accordance with Section 56341(d) of the Education Code. The individualized education program team shall take into account all the relevant material which is available on the pupil. **No single score or product of scores shall be used as the sole criterion for the decision of the individualized education program team as to the pupil's eligibility for special education.** The specific processes and procedures for implementation of these criteria shall be developed by each Special Education Local Plan Area and be included in the local plan pursuant to Section 56220(a) of the Education Code.

(a) **Definition of Hearing Impairment**. A pupil has a hearing impairment, whether permanent or fluctuating, which impairs the processing of linguistic information through hearing, even with amplification, and which adversely affects educational performance. Processing linguistic information includes speech and language reception and speech and language discrimination.

(b) **Definition of Hearing and Visual Impairment**. A pupil has concomitant hearing and visual impairments, the combination of which causes severe communication, developmental, and educational problems.

(c) **Definition of Language or Speech Disorder**. A pupil has a language or speech disorder as defined in Section 56333 of the Education Code, and it is determined that the pupil's disorder meets one or more of the following criteria:

    (1) **Articulation Disorder.**

        (A) The pupil displays reduced intelligibility or an inability to use the speech mechanism which significantly interferes with communication and attracts adverse attention. Significant interference in communication occurs when the pupil's production of single or multiple speech sounds on a developmental scale of articulation competency is below that expected for his or her chronological age or developmental level, and which adversely affects educational performance.

        (B) A pupil does not meet the criteria for an articulation disorder if the sole assessed disability is an abnormal swallowing pattern.

    (2) **Abnormal Voice**. A pupil has an abnormal voice which is characterized by persistent, defective voice quality, pitch, or loudness.

    (3) **Fluency Disorders**. A pupil has a fluency disorder when the flow of verbal expression including

rate and rhythm adversely affects communication between the pupil and listener.

(4) **Language Disorder**. The pupil has an expressive or receptive language disorder when he or she meets one of the following criteria:

(A) The pupil scores at least 1.5 standard deviations below the mean, or below the 7th percentile, for his or her chronological age or developmental level on two or more standardized tests in one or more of the following areas of language development: morphology, syntax, semantics, or pragmatics. When standardized tests are considered to be invalid for the specific pupil, the expected language performance level shall be determined by alternative means as specified on the assessment plan, or

(B) The pupil scores at least 1.5 standard deviations below the mean or the score is below the 7th percentile for his or her chronological age or developmental level on one or more standardized tests in one of the areas listed in subsection (A) and displays inappropriate or inadequate usage of expressive or receptive language as measured by a representative spontaneous or elicited language sample of a minimum of fifty utterances. The language sample must be recorded or transcribed and analyzed, and the results included in the assessment report. If the pupil is unable to produce this sample, the language, speech, and hearing specialist shall document why a fifty utterance sample was not obtainable and the contexts in which attempts were made to elicit the sample. When standardized tests are considered to be invalid for the specific pupil, the expected language performance level shall be determined by alternative means as specified in the assessment plan.

(d) **Definition of Visual Impairment**. A pupil has a visual impairment which, even with correction, adversely affects a pupil's educational performance.

(e) **Definition of Orthopedic Impairment**. A pupil has a severe orthopedic impairment which adversely affects the pupil's educational performance. Such orthopedic impairments include impairments caused by congenital anomaly, impairments caused by disease, and impairments from other causes.

(f) **Definition of Acute Health Problems**. A pupil has limited strength, vitality or alertness, due to chronic or acute health problems, including but not limited to a heart condition, cancer, leukemia, rheumatic fever, chronic kidney disease, cystic fibrosis, severe asthma, epilepsy, lead poising, diabetes, tuberculosis and other communicable infectious diseases, and hematological disorders such as sickle cell anemia and hemophilia which adversely affects a pupil's educational performance. In accordance with Section 5626(e) of the Education Code, such physical disabilities shall not be temporary in nature as defined by Section 3001(v).

(g) **Definition of Autistic-Like Behaviors**. A pupil exhibits any combination of the following autistic-like behaviors, to include but not limited to:

   (1) **Oral Language Deficit**. An inability to use oral language for appropriate communication.

   (2) **Social Interaction Deficit**. A history of extreme withdrawal or relating to people inappropriately and continued impairment in social interaction from infancy through early childhood.

(3) **Sameness Obsession**. An obsession to maintain sameness.

(4) **Objects Deficit**. Extreme preoccupation with objects or inappropriate use of objects or both.

(5) **Control Deficits**. Extreme resistance to controls.

(6) **Mannerism and Pattern Deficit.** Displays peculiar motoric mannerisms and motility patterns.

(7) **Ritualistic Behavior Deficit**. Self-stimulating, ritualistic behavior.

(h) **Definition of Autistic-Like Behaviors with Other Deficits**. A pupil has significantly below average general intellectual functioning existing concurrently with deficits in adaptive behavior and manifested during the developmental period, which adversely affect a pupil's educational performance.

(i) **Definition of Serious Emotional Disturbance**. Because of a serious emotional disturbance, a pupil exhibits one or more of the following characteristics over a long period of time and to a marked degree, which adversely affect educational performance:

(1) **Undefined Inability to Learn**. An inability to learn which cannot be explained by intellectual, sensory, or health factors.

(2) **Poor Social Relationships**. An inability to build or maintain satisfactory interpersonal relationships with peers and teachers.

(3) **Inappropriate Behavior or Feelings**. Inappropriate types of behavior or feelings under normal circumstances exhibited in several situations.

(4) **Depressed Mood.** A general pervasive mood of unhappiness or depression.

(5) **Aversion to School or Personal Problems**. A tendency to develop physical symptoms or fears associated with personal or school problems.

(j) **Definition of Language Deficit**. A pupil has a disorder in one or more of the basic psychological processes involved in understanding or in using language, spoken or written, which may manifest itself in an impaired ability to listen, think, speak, read, write, spell, or do mathematical calculations, and has a severe discrepancy between intellectual ability and achievement in one or more of the academic areas specified in Section 56337(a) of the Education Code. For the purpose of Section 3030(j):

(1) **Nature of Psychological Processes**. Basic psychological processes include attention, visual processing, auditory processing, sensory-motor skills, cognitive abilities including association, conceptualization and expression.

(2) **Nature of Intellectual Ability**. Intellectual ability includes both acquired learning and learning potential and shall be determined by a systematic assessment of intellectual functioning.

(3) **Nature of Scholastic Achievement**. The level of achievement includes the pupil's level of competence in materials and subject matter explicitly taught in school and shall be measured by standardized achievement tests.

(4) **IEP Evaluation and Control**. The decision as to whether or not a severe discrepancy exists shall be made by the individualized education program team, including assessment personnel in accordance with Section 56341(d), which takes into account all

relevant material which is available on the pupil. No single score or product of scores, test or procedure shall be used as the sole criterion for the decisions of the individualized education program team as to the pupil's eligibility for special education.

In determining the existence of a severe discrepancy, the individualized education program team shall use the following procedures:

(A) When standardized tests are considered to be valid for a specific pupil, a severe discrepancy is demonstrated by: first, converting into common standard scores, using a mean of 100 and standard deviation of 15, the achievement test score and the ability test score to be compared; second, computing the difference between these common standard scores; and third, comparing this computed difference to the standard criterion which is the product of 1.5 multiplied by the standard deviation of the distribution of computed differences of students taking these achievement and ability tests.

A computed difference which equals or exceeds this standard criterion, adjusted by one standard error of measurement, the adjustment not to exceed 4 common standard score points, indicates a severe discrepancy when such discrepancy is corroborated by other assessment data which may include other tests, scales, instruments, observations and work samples, as appropriate.

(B) When standardized tests are considered to be invalid for a specific pupil, the discrepancy shall be measured by alternative means as specified on the assessment plan.

(C) If the standardized tests do not reveal a severe discrepancy as defined in subparagraphs (A) or (B) above, the individualized education program team may find that a severe discrepancy does exist, provided that the team documents in a written report that the severe discrepancy between ability and achievement exists as a result of a disorder in one or more of the basic psychological processes. The report shall include a statement of the area, the degree, and the basis and method used in determining the discrepancy.

The report shall contain information considered by the team which shall include, but not be limited to:

1. Data obtained from standardized assessment instruments;

2. Information provided by the parent;

3. Information provided by the pupil's present teacher;

4. Evidence of the pupil's performance in the regular and/or special education classroom obtained from observations, work samples, and group test scores;

5. Consideration of the pupil's age, particularly for young children; and

6. Any additional relevant information.

(5) **Not Due to Limited School Exposure**. The discrepancy shall not be primarily the result of limited school experience or poor school attendance.

5 CCR 3052 — Designated Positive Behavioral Interventions.

(a) **Designated Positive Behavioral Interventions**. General Provisions.

(1) **Behavioral Intervention Case Manager And IEP Team Develop**. An IEP team shall facilitate and supervise all assessment, intervention, and evaluation activities related to an individual's behavioral intervention plan. When the behavioral intervention plan is being developed, the IEP team shall be expanded to include the behavioral intervention case manager with documented training in behavior analysis including positive behavioral intervention(s), qualified personnel knowledgeable of the student's health needs, and others as described in Education Code section 56341(b)(6). The behavioral intervention case manager is not intended to be a new staff person and may be an existing staff member trained in behavior analysis with an emphasis on positive behavioral interventions.

(2) **Only Used Appropriately By Competent Personnel**. Behavioral intervention plans shall only be implemented by, or be under the supervision of, staff with documented training in behavior analysis, including the use of positive behavioral interventions. Such interventions shall only be used to replace specified maladaptive behavior(s) with alternative acceptable behavior(s) and shall never be used solely to eliminate maladaptive behavior(s).

(3) **Based Upon Functional Analysis Assessment and Included in IEP**. Behavioral intervention plans shall be based upon a functional analysis assessment, shall be specified in the IEP, and shall be used only in a systematic manner in accordance

with the provisions of this section.

(4) **Not Substitute for Behavioral Intervention Plans**. Behavioral emergency interventions shall not be used as a substitute for behavioral intervention plans.

(5) **Cannot Cause Pain or Trauma**. The elimination of any maladaptive behavior does not require the use of intrusive behavioral interventions that cause pain or trauma.

(6) **Strive for Consistency**. To the extent possible, behavioral intervention plans shall be developed and implemented in a consistent manner appropriate to each of the individual's life settings.

(b) **Functional Analysis Assessments**. A functional analysis assessment must be conducted by, or be under the supervision of a person who has documented training in behavior analysis with an emphasis on positive behavioral interventions. A functional analysis assessment shall occur after the IEP team finds that instructional/behavioral approaches specified in the student's IEP have been ineffective. Nothing in this section shall preclude a parent or legal guardian from requesting a functional analysis assessment pursuant to the provisions of Education Code sections 56320 et seq.

Functional analysis assessment personnel shall gather information from three sources: direct observation, interviews with significant others, and review of available data such as assessment reports prepared by other professionals and other individual records. Prior to conducting the assessment, parent notice and consent shall be given and obtained pursuant to Education Code section 56321.

(1) **Included in Functional Assessment**. A functional analysis assessment procedure shall include all of the following:

(A) **Observation of Objectionable Behavior**. Systematic observation of the occurrence of the targeted behavior for an accurate definition and description of the frequency, duration, and intensity;

(B) **Events Preceding Behavior.** Systematic observation of the immediate antecedent events associated with each instance of the display of the targeted inappropriate behavior;

(C) **Consequences of Behavior**. Systematic observation and analysis of the consequences following the display of the behavior to determine the function the behavior serves for the individual, i.e., to identify the specific environmental or physiological outcomes produced by the behavior. The communicative intent of the behavior is identified in terms of what the individual is either requesting or protesting through the display of the behavior;

(D) **Environment Influencing Behavior**. Ecological analysis of the settings in which the behavior occurs most frequently. Factors to consider should include the physical setting, the social setting, the activities and the nature of instruction, scheduling, the quality of communication between the individual and staff and other students, the degree of independence, the degree of participation, the amount and quality of social interaction, the degree of choice, and the variety of activities;

(E) **Health And Mental Factors Affecting**. Review of records for health and medical factors which may influence behaviors (e.g. medication levels, sleep cycles, health, diet); and

(F) **Previously Effective Interventions**. Review of the history of the behavior to include the effectiveness of previously used behavioral interventions.

(2) **Functional Analysis Assessment Reports.** Following the assessment, a written report of the assessment results shall be prepared and a copy shall be provided to the parent. The report shall include all of the following:

(A) **Analytical Description Of Behavior**. A description of the nature and severity of the targeted behavior(s) in objective and measurable terms;

(B) **Description Events Preceding Behavior**. A description of the targeted behavior(s) that includes baseline data and an analysis of the antecedents and consequences that maintain the targeted behavior, and a functional analysis of the behavior across all appropriate settings in which it occurs;

(C) **Description Of Alternate Behaviors**. A description of the rate of alternative behaviors, their antecedents and consequences; and

(D) **Recommendations For IEP**. Recommendations for consideration by the IEP team which may include a proposed plan as specified in section 3001(g).

(c) **IEP Team Meeting.** Upon completion of the functional analysis assessment, an IEP team meeting shall be held to review results and, if necessary, to develop a behavioral intervention plan, as defined in section 3001(g) of these regulations. The IEP team shall include the behavioral intervention case manager. The behavioral intervention plan shall become a part of the IEP and shall be written with sufficient detail so as to direct the implementation of the plan.

(d) **Intervention**. Based upon the results of the functional analysis assessment, positive programming for behavioral intervention may include the following:

(1) **Altering Events Preceding Behavior.** Altering the identified antecedent event to prevent the occurrence of the behavior (e.g., providing choice, changing the setting, offering variety and a meaningful curriculum, removing environmental pollutants such as excessive noise or crowding, establishing a predictable routine for the individual);

(2) **Teaching Proper Behavioral Responses**. Teaching the individual alternative behaviors that produce the same consequences as the inappropriate behavior (e.g., teaching the individual to make requests or protests using socially acceptable behaviors, teaching the individual to participate with alternative communication modes as a substitute for socially unacceptable attention-getting behaviors, providing the individual with activities that are physically stimulating as alternatives for stereotypic, self-stimulatory behaviors);

(3) **Teaching Self-Actualizing, Adaptive Behavior.** Teaching the individual adaptive behaviors (e.g., choice-making, self-management, relaxation techniques, and general skill development) which ameliorate negative conditions that promote the display of inappropriate behaviors; and

(4) **Adapting Consequences**. Manipulating the consequences for the display of targeted inappro-

priate behaviors and alternative, acceptable behaviors so that it is the alternative behaviors that more effectively produce desired outcomes (i.e., positively reinforcing alternative and other acceptable behaviors and ignoring or redirecting unacceptable behaviors).

(e) **Acceptable Responses**. When the targeted behavior(s) occurs, positive response options shall include, but are not limited to one or more of the following:

(1) the behavior is ignored, but not the individual;

(2) the individual is verbally or verbally and physically redirected to an activity;

(3) the individual is provided with feedback (e.g., "You are talking too loudly");

(4) the message of the behavior is acknowledged (e.g., "You are having a hard time with your work"); or

(5) a brief, physical prompt is provided to interrupt or prevent aggression, self-abuse, or property destruction.

(f) **Evaluation of the Behavioral Intervention Plan Effectiveness**. Evaluation of the effectiveness of the behavioral intervention plan shall be determined through the following procedures:

(1) **Documented Baseline Measurements**. Baseline measure of the frequency, duration, and intensity of the targeted behavior, taken during the functional analysis assessment. Baseline data shall be taken across activities, settings, people, and times of the day. The baseline data shall be used as a standard against which to evaluate intervention effectiveness;

(2) **Continuous Monitoring.** Measures of the frequency, duration, and intensity of the targeted behavior shall be taken after the behavioral intervention plan is implemented at scheduled intervals determined by the IEP team. These measures shall also be taken across activities, settings, people, and times of the day, and may record the data in terms of time spent acting appropriately rather than time spent engaging in the inappropriate behavior;

(3) **Written Documentation.** Documentation of program implementation as specified in the behavioral intervention plan (e.g., written instructional programs and data, descriptions of environmental changes); and

(4) **Evaluate And Review Effectiveness.** Measures of program effectiveness will be reviewed by the teacher, the behavioral intervention case manager, parent or care provider, and others as appropriate at scheduled intervals determined by the IEP team. This review may be conducted in meetings, by telephone conference, or by other means, as agreed upon by the IEP team.

(5) **Modification Through IEP.** If the IEP team determines that changes are necessary to increase program effectiveness, the teacher and behavioral intervention case manager shall conduct additional functional analysis assessments and, based on the outcomes, shall propose changes to the behavioral intervention plan.

(g) **Modifications without IEP Team Meeting.** Minor modifications to the behavioral intervention plan can be made by the behavioral intervention case manager and the parent or parent representative. If the case manager is unavailable, a qualified designee who meets the training requirements of subdivision (a)(1) shall participate in such modifications. Each modification or change shall be addressed in the behavioral intervention plan provided that the parent, or parent representative, is notified of the need and is able to review the existing program evaluation data prior to implementing the modification or change. Parents shall be informed of their right to question any modification to the plan through the IEP procedures.

(h) **Contingency Behavioral Intervention Plans**. Nothing in this section is intended to preclude the IEP team from initially developing the behavioral intervention plan in sufficient detail to include schedules for altering specified procedures, or the frequency or duration of the procedures, without the necessity for reconvening the IEP team. Where the intervention is to be used in multiple settings, such as the classroom, home and job sites, those personnel responsible for implementation in the other sites must also be notified and consulted prior to the change.

(i) **Emergency Interventions**. Emergency interventions may only be used to control unpredictable, spontaneous behavior which poses clear and present danger of serious physical harm to the individual or others and which cannot be immediately prevented by a response less restrictive than the temporary application of a technique used to contain the behavior.

(1) **Emergency Limited to Emergencies**. Emergency interventions shall not be used as a substitute for the systematic behavioral intervention plan that is designed to change, replace, modify, or eliminate a targeted behavior.

(2) **Can Use Only Approved Emergency Interventions.** Whenever a behavioral emergency occurs, only behavioral emergency interventions approved by the SELPA may be used.

(3)· **Emergency Not Extended Or Expanded Needlessly.** No emergency intervention shall be employed for longer than is necessary to contain the behavior. Any situation which requires prolonged use of an emergency intervention shall require staff to seek assistance of the school site administrator or law enforcement agency, as applicable to the situation.

(4) **Prohibited Interventions**. Emergency interventions may not include:

(A) **Approved Locked Seclusion**. Locked seclusion, unless it is in a facility otherwise licensed or permitted by state law to use a locked room;

(B) **Total Limb Immobilization**. Employment of a device or material or objects which simultaneously immobilize all four extremities, except that techniques such as prone containment may be used as an emergency intervention by staff trained in such procedures; and

(C) **Reasonable And Necessary Force**. An amount of force that exceeds that which is reasonable and necessary under the circumstances.

(5) **Requires Prompt Notification And Documentation**. To prevent emergency interventions from being used in lieu of planned, systematic behavioral interventions, the parent and residential care provider, if appropriate, shall be notified within one school day whenever an emergency intervention is used or serious property damage occurs. A "Behavioral Emergency Report" shall immediately be completed and maintained in the individual's

file. The report shall include all of the following:

(A) The name and age of the individual;

(B) The setting and location of the incident;

(C) The name of the staff or other persons involved [in the intervention];

(D) A description of the incident and the emergency intervention used, and whether the individual is currently engaged in any systematic behavioral intervention plan; and

(E) Details of any injuries sustained by the individual or others, including staff, as a result of the incident.

(6) **Behavioral Emergency Reports Reviewed.** All "Behavioral Emergency Reports" shall immediately be forwarded to, and reviewed by, a designated responsible administrator.

(7) **If No Behavioral Intervention Plan Then Prompt Evaluation For Disability**. Anytime a "Behavioral Emergency Report" is written regarding an individual who does not have a behavioral intervention plan, the designated responsible administrator shall, within two days, schedule an IEP team meeting to review the emergency report, to determine the necessity for a functional analysis assessment, and to determine the necessity for an interim behavioral intervention plan. The IEP team shall document the reasons for not conducting an assessment and/or not developing an interim plan.

(8) **If Incident Where Behavioral Intervention Plan Then Prompt Evaluation For IEP.** Anytime a "Behavioral Emergency Report" is written

regarding an individual who has a behavioral intervention plan, any incident involving a previously unseen serious behavior problem or where a previously designed intervention is not effective should be referred to the IEP team to review and determine if the incident constitutes a need to modify the plan.

(9) **SELPAs Maintain Overall Data**. "Behavioral Emergency Report" data shall be collected by SELPAs which shall report annually the number of Behavioral Emergency Reports to the CDE and the Advisory Committee on Special Education.

(j) **SELPA Plan**. The local plan of each SELPA shall include procedures governing the systematic use of behavioral interventions and emergency interventions. These procedures shall be part of the SELPA local plan.

(1) **Availability Of SELPA Plan**. Upon adoption, these procedures shall be available to all staff members and parents whenever a behavioral intervention plan is proposed.

(2) **Included In SELPA Plan**. At a minimum, the plan shall include:

(A) **Type Training And Qualifications Of Personnel**. The qualifications and training of personnel to be designated as behavioral intervention case managers, which shall include training in behavior analysis with an emphasis on positive behavioral interventions, who will coordinate and assist in conducting the functional analysis assessments and the development of the behavioral intervention plans;

(B) **Training And Qualification Of Personnel.** The qualifications and training required of personnel who will participate in the implementation of the behavioral intervention plans; which shall include training in positive behavioral interventions;

(C) **Type Special Training Needed**. Special training that will be required for the use of emergency behavioral interventions and the types of interventions requiring such training; and

(D) **Procedures Approved.** Approved behavioral emergency procedures.

(k) **Nonpublic School Policy.** Nonpublic schools and agencies, serving individuals pursuant to Education Code section 56365 et seq., shall develop policies consistent with those specified in subdivision (i) of this section.

(l) **Prohibitions**. No public education agency, or nonpublic school or agency serving individuals pursuant to Education Code section 56365 et seq., may authorize, order, consent to, or pay for any of the following interventions, or any other interventions similar to or like the following:

(1) **No Physical Pain**. Any intervention that is designed to, or likely to, cause physical pain;

(2) **No Noxious, Etc. To Face**. Releasing noxious, toxic or otherwise unpleasant sprays, mists, or substances in proximity to the individual's face;

(3) **No Deprivation of Necessities**. Any intervention which denies adequate sleep, food, water, shelter, bedding, physical comfort, or access to bathroom facilities;

(4) **No Actions Causing Excessive Emotional Trauma**. Any intervention which is designed to

subject, used to subject, or likely to subject the individual to verbal abuse, ridicule or humiliation, or which can be expected to cause excessive emotional trauma;

(5) **No Excessive Physical Restraints.** Restrictive interventions which employ a device or material or objects that simultaneously immobilize all four extremities, including the procedure known as prone containment, except that prone containment or similar techniques may be used by trained personnel as a limited emergency intervention pursuant to subdivision (i);

(6) **Unapproved Locked Seclusion.** Locked seclusion, except pursuant to subdivision (i)(4)(A);

(7) **Inadequate Supervision Of Interventions.** Any intervention that precludes adequate supervision of the individual; and

(8) **Depriving One Of Child's Five Senses.** Any intervention which deprives the individual of one or more of his or her senses.

(m) **Due Process Hearings.** The provisions of this chapter related to functional analysis assessments and the development and implementation of behavioral intervention plans are subject to the due process hearing procedures specified in Education Code section 56501 et seq. No hearing officer may order the implementation of a behavioral intervention that is otherwise prohibited by this section, by SELPA policy, or by any other applicable statute or regulation.